SUFFICIENT TO **STAND**

Human Drama
with
Divine Design

Friends
Community Church

Published in Beaverton, Oregon, by Good Catch Publishing.
www.goodcatchpublishing.com
V1.1

Printed in the United States of America

TABLE OF CONTENTS

"... he had of me all he could have; I made him just and right, sufficient to have stood, though free to fall."

John Milton, *Paradise Lost*

ACKNOWLEDGEMENTS

I would like to thank Pastor Jeff Wall for the hard work, prayer and faith he put into this book to make it a reality; Meadow Riedel for the vision she had from the beginning and the effort she put into making this book come to life; and the people of Friends Community Church for their boldness and vulnerability in telling the stories that comprise this compilation of real-life stories.

This book would not have been published without the amazing efforts of our project manager, Jennifer Wade. Her untiring resolve pushed this project forward and turned it into a stunning victory. Thank you for your great fortitude and diligence. I would also like to thank our invaluable proofreader, Melody Davis, for all the focus and energy she has put into perfecting our words. Lastly, I want to extend my gratitude to Meadow Riedel, who designed the beautiful cover of this book.

Daren Lindley
President and CEO
Good Catch Publishing

The book you are about to read is a compilation of authentic life stories.
All the facts are true, and all the events are real.
These storytellers have dealt with crisis, tragedy, abuse and neglect and have shared their most private moments, mess-ups and hang-ups in order for others to learn and grow from them.
In order to protect the identities of those involved in their pasts, the names of some storytellers have been withheld or changed.

INTRODUCTION

The promise of sufficiency is a powerful gift from God. We can find ourselves in circumstances where we feel anything but sufficient to deal with the issue at hand. Certainly one of the most challenging of these is confronting addiction in any one of its many forms.

Dr. Gerald May in *Grace and Addiction* calls these circumstances "attachments." It is a particularly graphic term when we consider its origin in old French, meaning "being nailed to." That is how it feels sometimes when we try unsuccessfully to rid ourselves of what Paul may have alluded to when he asked God to remove "the thorn from my flesh."

God's answer was one of sufficiency: "My grace is sufficient for you."

This was not a rebuff of Paul's prayer, but an answer, a direction. Paul's plaintiff description of the struggle in Romans 7:18 and following must ring true for many people and many Christians, as well. It certainly rings true for me. He cries out that, despite the will to do so, the good we want to do, we do not; and the evil we do not wish to do, we do. He describes "another law" in us, "warring against the law of my mind, and bringing me into captivity to the law of sin which is in [my flesh]."

The stories you will read in this book describe this war, describe this captivity. There is a profound helplessness, a

SUFFICIENT TO **STAND**

deep feeling of insufficiency when we confront something we *shouldn't*, but it is something we *can't help*. This is a war we cannot win until we call upon the Lord who took captivity captive. Dr. May calls grace "the invincible advocate of freedom." Christ was nailed to a cross so that we could overcome our "attachments."

That is the solution, but it is not easy. Especially for Christians, there exists a deep sense of shame in our addictions. Satan is yelling to us, "Fight it! You call yourself a Christian? You better beat this thing before you go to church with all those people who can control their behavior." Satan invented shame. The first thing Adam and Eve did upon eating of the forbidden fruit was to hide themselves from God, because they were naked. They were ashamed of their flesh. The warring had begun; the captivity had begun.

Original sin cast man out of the Garden of Eden, but more importantly, cast man out of the presence of God. There was no answer to the warring or to the captivity for mankind in general until the cross. "Once and for all," the sacrifice of Jesus Christ gave us sufficiency through his grace.

I am so thankful for the testimonies of the members of Friends Church, so thankful for the attitude of our congregation and our pastor, who says, "If you are overcome — come over."

Learn from each other the freedom and the empowerment of God's grace. Be inspired by others who are winning the war, who are enjoying the freedom, knowing you

INTRODUCTION

will need to be there for them, our brothers and sisters in Christ, our fellow strugglers.

Mark Hamilton, President
University of Alaska

A SKATEBOARDER'S HIGH ON LIFE
THE STORY OF ERIK SETTERBERG
WRITTEN BY DIANNE CHRISTNER

Amazingly, the skater with a skull on his shirt invited me — a sixth-grade nobody — into his cool world.

"Hey, dude, wanna come with us?"

The kid bent deep, popped an "ollie" on his board and landed with a roll. He was with a bunch of neighborhood kids I admired, older kids my brother knew and better skaters than me.

"Where?" I asked, trying to act bad even though a surge of electrifying current assured me this insider experienced life in a thrilling way. More than anything, I craved his acceptance.

"Gonna steal some guns out of an apartment on the other side of town."

My blood stirred with images of tattooed, muscular, leather-clad men on powerful bikes, and the idea that this kid would dare to hoist their guns made him incredibly bad. A small voice in my head belonging to my ordained-minister parents objected — *stealing is a sin* — but I craved this kid's approval. My parents' ideals would grow moss on my feet, while this fleeting opportunity could fulfill my lust for adventure.

I shrugged. "Sure, I'll go."

SUFFICIENT TO **STAND**

An empty driveway led up to an unlit house with some of its shades drawn tight. One of the skaters asked me to guard the outside, while he and the others jumped the fence. My heart lurched at the sound of shattering glass. No hide-and-seek game, this was real stuff. I cheered when my friends reappeared, their arms laden with guns, liquor and porn magazines. But best of all, I felt an exhilarating rush to think we hadn't gotten caught. In exaltation, I ran with them to safety.

That night, I forsook my innocence, hanging with these older teens and sharing their secret. I offered them the use of our backyard clubhouse, where my brother — who was 18 months older than me — was camped out for the summer. My brother was surprised, but he invited us in. With rap music blaring in the background, we kicked back to drink liquor and rehash the robbery, while examining the magazines and guns they would sell at the high school.

The next weekend, we played basketball at a vacant house in the neighborhood. A few of the kids broke into a nearby house and stole some alcohol. This time, the cops came. I'd been taught not to lie to authority figures, so I squealed on the kids. The policemen handcuffed them and hauled them off to jail, while my brother and I sat on my front porch and cried. My dad lectured me and grounded us for the rest of the summer. My only option was to hang out at Joel's Place, a faith-based youth center in Fairbanks, Alaska, founded and directed by my parents. I thought hanging out at Joel's Place would be a drag, but some interesting kids actually hung out there, and one of them introduced me to cigarettes.

Bad-Mouthed Class Clown

I started middle school, and as the leaves turned brown, withered and fell, so did my budding reputation. My brother grew jealous of my involvement with his friends and spread the lie that I was gay. To disprove this, I snuck out my window and met with girls on a frequent basis. Through these sexual relationships and by smoking, I attained the popularity I craved among my classmates.

One day in seventh grade, I strutted into class with my skateboard in my hand. I noticed this cute girl across the room, clacked my skateboard on the ground and confidently questioned, "What's up, girl?" She smiled and giggled, and several students tittered. I gave her a flirtatious glance and she blushed. About half of the other students shifted their gazes away from the teacher to follow our antics.

The lecture stopped, and I could feel my classmates' gazes, knowing the teacher was spearing me with a quelling look. But in order to maintain my growing reputation as a badass, I ignored him.

I winked, slowly ran my gaze over her short red skirt that barely covered her shapely legs and blurted out, "Hot outfit."

She uncrossed and crossed her legs again. My guy friends leered.

SUFFICIENT TO **STAND**

The teacher cleared his throat. "Whenever you're ready to settle down, Erik, we'll continue."

"Whatever." I shrugged and slumped lower in my chair.

He resumed his lecture.

I straightened and waved my pencil in the air to capture the girl's attention.

Several of my classmates giggled.

Cupping my mouth with my hands, I lipped, "Boring."

"Erik, be quiet," the teacher warned.

"Whatever." I tilted my chair on two legs and yawned real big with outstretched arms. My chair legs then banged back onto the floor, and I mumbled, "Boring."

"That's it. Take your mouth to the principal's office."

"Why? All I did was yawn."

"You're disruptive." He scribbled out a message for me to give the principal. "Go on, get out."

I kicked my chair, and it toppled over. "This is crap!" I shrugged my shoulders, gave the girl another wink and ambled out, giving the door a loud slam. Then I strutted to the principal's office with an inward smile, knowing I'd elevated my bad-mouth, class-clown reputation a notch. The principal called it flagrant disrespect — an admirable trait to my peers.

Caught Red-Handed

In eighth grade, an old friend, three years older and a role model to me, moved permanently to Fairbanks. He and a kid from Joel's Place taught me how to smoke weed. The second time, we smoked outside the skate park. Amazed, I no longer viewed drugs as horrific as the D.A.R.E. program portrayed them. The unhealthy aspects of drugs faded into the recesses of my mind, while weed's cool image dominated my thinking. I often lied to my parents to stay out of trouble. My friends pooled money to buy weed and smoke it in our clubhouse, where we'd sneak girls inside. Smoking weed relaxed us and filled us with good humor and high spirits, creating memories of fun times to brag about at school.

A week before entering high school, I used my lawn-mowing money to buy $50 worth of weed. During orientation and the first two weeks of my freshman year, I smoked weed with my friends during break, which created a foggy, confusing existence in which I drifted in and out of class.

One such day, I was absentmindedly munching on a slice of pizza during class, when a shadow appeared at my right shoulder, and I looked up.

The teacher gazed down her long nose at me. Her hand snapped out. "I'll take that. Lunch break is over." I heard her heels clacking back to her desk.

Squinting, I saw my pizza gleaming at me from the top of a pile of homework papers. My stomach growled, and I scooted back my chair. Sauntering forward, I snatched the slice and bit into it hungrily.

"Thanks," I mumbled as the cheese strung loosely between the pizza and my mouth. With satisfaction, I strode

SUFFICIENT TO **STAND**

to my seat, slunk back down and closed my eyes to chew.

I heard an outbreak of laughter and opened my eyes in confusion.

She stood beside my desk again with her hands on her hips.

I gave a feeble, food-filled smile. "I'm hungry." I lifted up the half-eaten slice. "Want a bite?"

She left again, and the next thing I knew, a hand clutched my shoulder. "Wake up."

"What?"

The hall monitor gestured for me to go with him.

"What do you want?" I scraped my chair back to stand.

"Come with me."

Half-dazed, I followed him to the principal's office and gladly took a seat. There, I stretched out my legs and closed my 100-pound eyelids. When I awoke about an hour later, the assistant principal's breath whipped my head back and my gaze upward. "Come with me."

"Okay." I tilted my face away from hers and shrugged.

She stared at me from across her expansive desk. "What did you do at lunch today?"

I contorted my mouth, trying to remember. "Me and my friend . . . we went . . . to the science lab," I grinned, "to pick up our assignment sheet. The door was locked and the cafeteria was closed, and I went to my locker and found an apple and went to class."

"Take a seat in the hall again, while I check out your story."

My head clouded over, heavy with confusion. I didn't

care about the principal. I nodded and jerked.

Wasn't my first time.

I dozed for another hour or so before the head principal called my name.

"Mr. Setterberg." I blinked and remembered my fate. "Come in here."

"Yeah, I'll do that." I stood on tingling legs and stretched, then followed her into her office.

She asked the same stupid question. "What did you do at lunch today?"

I tried to remember what I'd told the assistant principal, but nothing came to me. With mild panic, I realized my mind remained blank. "What did I do?" I repeated, stalling. "Hmm." I tapped my knee and twisted my mouth. "Well, I …" An idea sprung to my mind. "I did math homework in the cafeteria. You can ask my friends, they'll vouch for me."

She tightened her lips, and then replied in a cold tone, "Is that a fact?" Next, my mom stepped into the room with a flushed face and wary expression. The principal invited her to sit beside me. She glanced over, sized up the situation and sighed.

"What's the deal? What happened?"

"Your son was caught eating and sleeping in class. He fabricated two different stories to explain his behavior. We want you to take him to get a urinalysis drug test to see if he's using weed."

My mom stood up, her nostrils flaring. "It doesn't take a rocket scientist to figure out if somebody's high or not!"

SUFFICIENT TO **STAND**

She slung her purse over her shoulder, grabbed me by the arm and marched me out of the office.

"Ouch. Let go." I shrugged away.

She snapped, "Go to your locker. Get your things and meet me back at the car — now!"

That day, my mom withdrew me from West Valley High and placed me in a private school.

At the private school, I couldn't use as many drugs, but another student bought me a pack of Newport cigarettes. They tasted great. Every night before bed, I'd sit on the roof to gaze at Fairbanks' city lights and smoke a cigarette. Eventually, I became addicted to them.

One day, that same kid and I decided to take a walk to a local mall to meet with my weed hookup. When we returned to school, someone must have smelled it or heard someone bragging about it because one of the teachers found out. I got kicked out of that school because of it.

Next, my mom homeschooled me. Every night, my dad lectured me on spiritual matters. However, my mind was closed to anything except smoking weed. I'd smoke it in my room with my window open. One day, I stole $50 from a car at Joel's Place. After that, I decided I didn't want to steal to buy weed, and so I started selling to support my smoking habit. The more people I hooked up, the more my reputation grew for offering the best stuff around. Pretty soon, everyone was coming to me to buy his weed.

A SKATEBOARDER'S HIGH

Selling to Support my Habit

My parents enrolled me at Hutchinson Career Center, where one day, I bought some weed by text messaging on my cell phone during class.

I raised my hand. "Can I get a bathroom pass?"

My teacher nodded, and I strode to his desk. Expressionless, he scribbled one and shoved it toward me.

I snatched it up and rushed through the nearly vacant halls, my heart hammering as I pushed against the bar and shouldered open an exit door. The seller grinned and took my money in exchange for a bag of weed, which I stashed between my boxers and low-riding pants. I'd taken as long of a break as I dared, so I hurried back to class.

I'd barely returned to my seat when the kid next to me barked out, "Who farted?" I cringed, while others wrinkled their noses and swatted the air in front of their faces. Some students recognized the smell and nodded their approval, but the teacher didn't do anything, and soon the bell rang.

At break, I rushed to the bathroom to check out the weed, then stuffed it back in my pants. As I was walking out, the principal entered. With my adrenalin racing, I hurried to my friend's locker, where I hid the weed in his coat until I could get it inside my own locker.

"I smell weed!" a kid yelled in the hall. My friend jammed his shoulder into the kid, and the kid staggered, the air rushing out of his lungs in a whoosh.

"Shut up!"

SUFFICIENT TO **STAND**

Gesturing with out-flung arms, the kid backed up. "Okay."

In the next class, my forehead beaded up in sweat, and I couldn't concentrate on anything except the principal checking my locker. Some kids claimed he had squirted deodorizing spray in the bathroom. He'd smelled the weed and thought someone had been smoking it. He'd seen me come out of the bathroom, too. So I asked for another bathroom pass, and I used it to transfer the weed from my locker to the girl's next to mine. Then I rested easy.

At lunch, I opened her locker and sold the weed in the hall. After lunch, the principal searched my locker. Although the weed was gone, he made me take a urinalysis. I passed it and was clean at school.

Ironically, the next week, I received three days of in-home suspension for smoking a cigarette in a friend's car at school. The day I got out, I bad-mouthed a teacher and received another in-home suspension. I ended up with nine straight days of I.H.S., but they didn't catch me selling or using drugs. I sold all year and never got caught.

The school, however, constantly called in my parents over my behavior — skipping classes and showing disrespect to teachers. My dad was disappointed with me that entire year, and we were all surprised when I ended the year with all the appropriate credits.

Cocaine

At the fast food place where I worked, people bought

and sold weed. A kid named Chris, who drove a nice sports car, gave me rides. I started using cocaine with him, either snorting it or dipping it with my finger and placing it on my tongue. One day, he joked, "I think in a month, my car'll be wrecked."

That's weird, I thought, wondering why he felt such a weird premonition. I shrugged. Maybe he just realized the risk of driving while under the influence.

About a month later, while hanging out one night, Chris asked, "Wanna drive?"

The previous night, we'd snorted cocaine and traces remained in our systems. Fingering my unlit weed and anticipating the smoke, I felt a little crazy. "Heck, yeah!"

Some girls in the backseat giggled as I got behind the wheel. I turned the key and revved the engine. A thrill tingled down my spine as the red car thrust us forward. On the Johansen Expressway, I accelerated to 90 miles per hour just as a distant traffic light turned red.

"Slow down," Chris warned.

About three football fields ahead, I spotted another car's lights. Adrenalin shot through me, and I sped up.

"Slow down," Chris repeated.

I stepped on it.

"Slow down!"

I felt the adrenalin spurting through my veins. I sped up even more, but then I got scared and started pumping the brakes. Realizing the car couldn't stop quickly enough, I panicked.

"Dude, I can't stop."

SUFFICIENT TO **STAND**

Chris's voice cracked out, "It'll be fine."

"No. It won't!" I yanked the emergency brake.

The girls in the backseat screamed as the car slid sideways across the icy expressway. Chris's eyes widened. "Dude, you're wrecking my car!"

We kept sliding. My hands jerked the wheel from side to side as I shouted, "No, I'm not, dude. Don't even worry about it."

Then the crash exploded in my ears as we struck the oncoming car in the middle of the intersection. Both cars spun off in opposite directions, and we nosedived into a snow bank.

I blacked out.

The first time I awoke, white-and-green-clad people poked and prodded me. The next time, I lay on a bed in a sterile hospital room with my parents staring at me with loving, worried expressions.

Later on, after I recovered, my mother told me I was diagnosed with drug-induced psychosis that night. She said I just kept repeating the same questions over and over and over again, because I could not hold onto a thought long enough to remember what I had just said. That night, God saved my life.

Stealing and Dealing

After the accident, my folks decided to home school me again. I continued smoking pot and using drugs. I stole skateboard decks from the skateboard shop by put-

A SKATEBOARDER'S HIGH

ting them half in my pants and half under my shirt and just walking out the door.

During the day, my mom gave me rides to Joel's Place and to work. I did my homework, often cheating and using the answer book. Sometimes, I actually did the work if it was an interesting subject. But I didn't sleep much while doing cocaine; it drove me to stay awake for days on end.

Chris forgave me. One morning, he called about 1 a.m.

"I've been checking out this car at UAF (University of Fairbanks). It has three 15-inch eclipse subwoofers."

"That's about $600 apiece," I stated, my hopes rising.

His voice lowered. "It has two sets of speakers."

"$400 apiece," I tallied.

"A deck adapter kit and the works."

"You wanna do it tonight?" My voice squeaked with expectation.

"Yeah. Meet me at the corner in half an hour."

Chris picked me up in his dad's 2006 Grand Prix around 2 a.m. The university was perched on a hilltop, overlooking Fairbanks in a queenly manner, but our intentions were far from noble. Chris drove up to the parking lot and wheeled in close to our target. We exchanged nervous glances, then positioned our bandanas and climbed out of the car, leaving our doors ajar. In a crouched position, little more than shadows in our black clothing, Chris pulled out a tool that glistened in the moonlight.

"Let's try to drill out the lock."

He struggled with the drill awhile, to no avail. With my

SUFFICIENT TO **STAND**

heart speeding as if I were high, I scoped the area. *If some-body drives by* . . . I imagined the worst. *Hurry . . . hurry,* but the lock wouldn't give. Chris grunted and raised a hammer.

The glass cracked, and he stuck his hand into the ragged hole and unlocked the door. I lunged into the car and, my hands keeping time to my throbbing pulse, un-screwed the expensive equipment and passed it to Chris, who layered it between blankets in the backseat of the Grand Prix.

Finally, we scrambled back into his dad's car and slammed the doors, letting out a sigh of relief.

"Sweet," I whispered happily.

Chris quietly put the car in gear, and we slunk away from the scene feeling pretty cool about ourselves.

"This was the cleanest, best job ever!" I gloated.

Smacking the steering wheel with both hands, Chris crooned, "I feel lucky!"

I soon discovered his intentions when we pulled into the parking lot of a liquor store. He had a hammer that he pulled out of the backseat, and we slowly left the car and approached the store. My chest was heaving with excite-ment as we stared through the window of the dark store. I cast a gaze down the dimly lit street at the *Closed* store signs and eerily empty sidewalks.

Unexpectedly, Chris wheeled round, swung the ham-mer hard and let it fly. It hurled through three panes of glass. He scampered to bust out the remaining shattered pieces with his shirt and scurried into the opening. But he'd missed a long, jagged shard, and it pierced his black t-shirt, goring an inch into his back.

"Ah!" he moaned. "I'm stuck!"

"Back out!"

He eased backwards until he worked himself free. "Ouch!" Then he charged through the window into the store.

I bolted to bring the car around, but it was locked, so I jogged back to the front of the store. Chris dashed by, juggling liquor bottles. I dove inside and grabbed two cases of beer, then returned for cigarettes. Chris squealed the car's tires, and I jumped inside.

"You're bleeding!" I yelled.

"But we didn't get caught."

"We never get caught," I beamed.

One day, Chris did get caught drinking and driving. He blacked in and out and drove his jeep into Chena Lakes. When he woke up, he was at a strange house with about 50 people, some cops and an ambulance clustered around. Someone called my house at 4 a.m. to see if I might have drowned. My parents were relieved I wasn't involved in the escapade. But Chris went to jail for DUI. This left me with the stolen stereo equipment.

I traded some of the equipment for a week's worth of cocaine, which was worth $700. The drug buzzed my brain to about 100 miles per hour and increased my heart rate until it nearly exploded. This lasted about 20 minutes. When I started to come down, I snorted another line. The reps kept the bad side effects away — the crazy depression and stomach pains.

At this point in my life, I loved my lifestyle, the adrenalin rush of dealing and stealing. I couldn't get enough of it.

But after a week, I'd run out of cocaine, so I went with a friend to smoke some weed in his truck.

"I need to blow my nose," I complained.

"Dude, we'll go to a gas station later."

"I need to go now."

My friend just sat there, stoned and stuck on stupid, so I shouldered open the door and jumped out of the truck onto the asphalt. I peeled off my coat and threw it inside, shivering in the frigid Alaska weather. Then I removed my white shirt and blew my nose for about five or 10 minutes. When I'd finished, I glanced at my shirt and froze in shock. The t-shirt was covered in blood. My heart panicked. Fear shot through my veins. It was the most disgusting, scarring event of my life as far as cocaine goes. I vowed I'd never snort again. I loved cocaine, but I couldn't keep snorting it. Something inside me died.

My friends suggested I try meth. I could smoke it, and I was good at smoking. But I'd tried it once before and hated it because it left me fatigued, stressed and gave me a nightmarish headache. But my friends encouraged me to give it another try, so I did. I smoked in my friend's truck, listening to rap music on a loud stereo system. We stayed up all night, and I decided to do some lines to continue my high. My brain buzzed, and I got into a little free styling, a little rapping and writing lyrics — a great experi-

A SKATEBOARDER'S HIGH

ence.

So, I continued to use and sell meth, staying awake for long periods of time all winter long. I felt guilty at Christmas when my folks gave me some sweet skating gear and a new snowboard. But I continued to steal and bragged to my friends how I never got caught.

One day, my parents got on my case because I stayed out all night. I decided not to come home at all after that, but they eventually persuaded me to attend a family meeting. At this meeting, my family members told me they didn't feel loved by me. It hurt, and the pain cut through layers of my hardened heart and calloused emotions. I felt broken by my family. Afterwards, I struggled. I realized the drugs I lived for were destroying me. My life was a facade, a giant cover up around my family. I used treacherous means to bed girls and steal, but I didn't know how to change ... or even if I wanted to change.

About a week later, I came home late. My dad, who had always treated me with respect no matter how much trouble I caused, started yelling.

"Erik, what are you doing?"

"What do you mean?"

"You're always coming home late, and I'm sick of it."

His tone was unusually angry, and that frightened me. "Why are you freakin' out? You never freak out on me."

His eyes darkened. "Shut your mouth, Erik. Just listen. You're being an idiot right now. You're never going to succeed in life."

I felt my jaw drop, and my eyes bugged.

SUFFICIENT TO **STAND**

Dad had never torn me down before.

"Look at the life you lead. I went out in the garage and saw all that stereo equipment." He threw his arms up in a desperate gesture. "You think I don't know about that? I've known for a long time." He shook his head and lowered his voice to a deadlier tone. "I just can't live with a kid who acts like you do anymore."

My mind frantically clawed at my options. I was still a kid until I turned 18. Dad bore a steady gaze at me, and I got the sense I was at a crossroads in my life. Either I chose him and everything he represented, or I chose to continue using drugs. Again, my emotions churned. "Screw it, Dad!" I swiped at my eyes with my sleeve. "Fine! I'll just call the cops right now." The tears gushed down my cheeks, and blindly, I punched at the numbers on my cell phone.

"I want to turn myself in," I sobbed. "I steal and do drugs, and I need to quit."

"Come on into the station, young man," the officer calmly stated.

My dad flung his arm around me, clasped me tight in a bear hug and, struggling with his own tears, walked me to the car. As we drove to the station, he spoke words of encouragement to me. I don't know why I chose the better path that night, except for the pain I'd felt when my dad rejected me for my behavior. So I wrote the officers a book about all my thefts and drug dealings, desperate to win back my dad's acceptance.

The court sentenced me to "sight and sound" — remaining within my parents' sight or within their hearing for 24 hours a day, seven days a week. But I had three months until that sentence went into effect.

I got stuck again at Joel's Place, and I needed to quit drugs, because in two weeks, I would have to endure a drug test. But the urge to get high overcame me, and I did use drugs one last time before my sentence went into effect. After that, I felt awful, and I knew I needed to make a change. The next day, I woke up and remembered the youth center's 24-hour prayer meeting had started the previous night.

A bunch of people at Joel's Place, including some of the kids I'd first started using drugs with, begged me to come downstairs so they could pray for me.

I shrugged. "Whatever."

A Christian band played music in the background, and my friends and family encircled me on the floor and placed their hands on my shoulders and back to show their caring support. Then, one by one, they prayed for me and my struggles. As they lifted their voices to plead on my behalf, my heart grieved and filled with love for them. My body shuddered, and I wept uncontrollably. Then, as my emotions grew calmer, a peace fell over me, and it seemed like God's presence had entered the room. His Spirit hovered over me and in me, and it was the most tangible experience I've ever had with God.

For two to three hours, we cried, laughed and had an amazing time. And God, in his goodness, set me free. I felt a great burden lift off me, and a bliss settled over me that

SUFFICIENT TO **STAND**

was better than any drug I had ever ingested. I believe God remolded my cardboard, cocaine-ruined nose. I believe he healed me from the inside out, and he even took away the desire to use drugs. These were things friends, counselors and physicians couldn't achieve; the complete change had to be explained by my God. There's no other reason that, in one prayer session, my drug obsession died and my body completely healed. God is the only physician that powerful or that strong.

Even though God removed my desire to use drugs, it took self-motivation to say no to my drug circle of friends and dealers. Thankfully, the court's sight and sound sentence kept me safe under my mom's supervision. The court assigned me to a female counselor for evaluation, and she signed a document stating I would most likely never use drugs again. An officer of the court asked me to choose a rehab treatment. I chose the Alaskan Military Youth Academy. The judge warned me if I was kicked out of it, I'd go straight to jail. I waited five months, and then one week before school started, I received verification that I could attend.

The school was like a boot camp with fake guns and homework, attended by many smoking, cussing sailors who talked in a filthy, negative and perverse language. However, God sent me my personal angel. Joey was a man in his 30s — a God-fearing man. While other students slept in their bunks, we'd go outside the dorms, and this amazing person would talk to me about God and life and feelings. He mentored me with his God-like behavior the whole time I attended the military academy.

The Alaskan Military Youth Academy was 500 miles from Fairbanks at Fort Richardson's Army base. My parents drove down once a month for the parent visitation. Most people with similar drug backgrounds barely scraped by, but I graduated with honors. I was on the director's list and wore that gold rope around my uniform as I walked across the stage of the huge gymnasium with its packed bleachers to collect my $300 check. It was my glory day. Needless to say, the court was pleased with my performance.

September 28, 2007, I received an e-mail that all seven misdemeanors I'd committed had been dropped, and my record was basically clean. Since graduating from the Alaskan Military Youth Academy, I've worked at Joel's Place at their new indoor skate park, and I am in my second semester at college. I'm working toward a two-year major in human services so that I can be an addictions counselor at the skate park.

It's been two years since I've used drugs, alcohol or cigarettes, and it ignites a thrill in my soul — greater than any drug could produce — to imagine where God will take me in the future.

The most amazing thing about Jesus is how he knew exactly when I was ready to change, then removed the negative elements from my life. He can do this for a person in the blink of an eye or over years and years of struggle and hardship; mine was the latter. But no matter how long it takes, what matters is I finally understand that Jesus is awesome, and I hope my life reflects his goodness and the strength of his power.

Today, my greatest desire and struggle is to remain sexually pure. At this point in my life, I've had to say no to girls. I've also repaid people and stores for items I've stolen and asked those I've hurt for forgiveness. I'm trusting Jesus to protect me from people who might seek revenge against me for refusing to buy and sell drugs.

I'm so thankful that God lifted me up out of Satan's dungeon. I've died to myself — my fleshly yearnings — and come alive for Jesus Christ. It's the best feeling in the world. I skateboard and snowboard for God, to reflect his love. Everything I do is now for him. I'm not trying to stay off drugs anymore; I'm free from them. And now I just want to speak life to everyone I meet, especially the kids at Joel's Place, to who I am a big brother and a mentor.

RECOVERING MY MANHOOD
THE STORY OF JOE
WRITTEN BY ANGELA PRUSIA

I capped my pen and stared at the list of names I'd recorded: Lisa, Rachel, Tory, Stephanie, Brittany, Jennifer, Malory, Kendra and Dena — every girl I ever liked who rejected me.

Am I that much of a loser? I'm in shape, and people tell me I'm good-looking. What is it? I can't change my basic personality; I'm analytical and sensitive. Does that turn girls off?

"I don't get it," I told God. "I thought you said I was too passive. You showed me that a girl's deepest desire is to know she's worth pursuing. So why doesn't Dena want anything to do with me?"

Silence.

I wadded up the list and threw it in the trash. No wonder I had a secret fear of girls.

Did they know the pain they inflicted when they hardly acknowledged my existence?

"If you're going to give me dating advice, God, why let me get burned again?"

More silence.

Anger churned inside me, competing with the pain. "Fine," I muttered "why won't you provide me with what I need? I can't live like this anymore. If I'm going to have my needs met, I'm going to have to do it myself since you aren't responding." I punched in Danny's phone number.

"Hey," I forced myself to sound upbeat. "You want to come over?"

"I'll be right over." Danny's voice was deep, inviting.

I took a shower, resolving to let things get as far as I dared — which they did.

I'd struggled with homosexual feelings all my life, but this was the first time I'd really acted on my fantasies. I'd pushed the boundaries a lot — deriving pleasure from wrestling around with the guys or hugs from my male friends.

Sometimes when I thought about my fear of girls, I wondered if an early childhood experience traumatized me.

***

"You kids go outside." My babysitter was cleaning up after lunch.

"Let's make a tent," Ashley, my babysitter's oldest daughter, suggested.

Her sister Mandy ran for a blanket. "We can put it over the swing set."

We positioned the blanket, using the teeter-totter swing to anchor each side.

"Cool," Ashley murmured. She lifted the edge of the blanket and disappeared inside.

Mandy and I followed. The blanket enfolded us like a

cocoon.

"It's our own secret world," Ashley whispered.

Our imaginations ran wild as we entertained adventures in faraway lands.

Soon, Ashley got bored and left to go play something else. I found myself alone with Mandy under the tent.

"You ever want a sister?" Mandy asked.

I shrugged. "Maybe." My brother was a few years younger than me, and my baby brother was just a speck in my parents' eye. "Do you want a brother?" I asked.

"Mom says boys are different than girls." Mandy smiled like she knew something I didn't.

Duh. I was 6; you know things like this already.

"She said boys go potty different than girls."

Double duh.

"Have you ever seen a girl naked?"

My eyes got big. "No," I shook my head.

"I've never seen a boy, either."

For some reason, my palms started to sweat.

"I'll show you mine if you show me yours," Mandy whispered.

"You first."

Mandy shook her head. "At the same time."

The two of us unzipped our jeans and let them fall to the ground. My mouth dropped open as I stared at Mandy. I hurried to pull up my pants, knowing we'd committed the forbidden.

Somehow, my parents discovered what we'd done.

"You know what you did was wrong," my mom

scolded seriously and deliberately. I sat on the table, my legs dangling over the side. I bit my lip, trying to hold back the tears.

"Girls need to be treated with the utmost respect." My dad's voice left no uncertainty in my mind.

I kicked my feet back and forth — anything to avoid thinking about the topic. My parents lectured me for half an hour, condemning my curiosity and emphasizing how what I did was wrong.

I'm not sure why the incident seared my memory like a branding iron, except that I was extremely sensitive. Years later, I observed girls from a distance, seeing them as objects of purity I was not allowed to touch.

Growing up, I always felt like the black sheep of the family. I was more interested in music than sports. Where my younger two brothers connected with our father, I felt estranged. I longed for him to affirm me, but he did little to encourage my sense of masculinity. I never told anyone, but I feared I didn't have what it took to be a man.

When my dad took some time with us boys, I never quite knew how to relate.

"Position yourself like this," my dad squared my brother's shoulders, "and you'll be able to swing easier."

Everett gripped the baseball bat, waiting for Dad to return to our makeshift pitcher's mound.

"Batter up," Dad called. He tossed the ball to my brother.

Crack. The ball made contact with the bat, and Everett shrieked, "I hit it!"

RECOVERING MY MANHOOD

"Run. Don't just stand there," my dad laughed.

I watched them at a distance, wanting to join in the fun, but not sure of my abilities. I wasn't athletic like Everett. He was the go-getter; I was more reserved.

"You want to play with us?" my dad called out.

I shook my head. "Nah."

I'm not good enough.

My dad turned back to Everett with a look of disappointment. I went inside, wishing my dad knew I needed his encouragement; I longed to know he believed in me.

My father worked the swing shift at the post office, so I didn't see him much during the week except before school — which wasn't a lot of time. Weekends weren't any better; he always seemed grumpy.

"Turn off the TV," my dad yelled.

"But it's Saturday," I groaned.

"Which means you need to get the lawn mowed and wash the cars."

I knew better than to argue. It's not like we'd do anything together, anyway. Dad didn't understand my love for music anymore than I understood his passion for things like sports and cars.

I started the mower. If I got done with everything, maybe I'd get to hang out with my best friend, Patrick.

"How come you didn't return my call?" I asked Patrick over the phone later.

"Something came up," he muttered.

I pressed him further. I'd learned to manipulate people well — probably something I learned from my mother. If

45

you controlled the situation the right way, people would play into your hand.

"You went to Jack's house, didn't you?" I called his bluff.

"So? Big deal."

My ears burned. It was a big deal to me. Jack and I weren't friends, so I felt left out when Patrick chose him over me.

"I like you, Joe, but I need some space," Patrick blurted out.

"Space?" I furrowed my brows.

"Yeah, space. I can't even hang out with my other friends without you getting mad."

I wanted to argue, but he was right. "You kinda smother a person."

Patrick might as well have stabbed me in the back; the wound hurt as much. Didn't Patrick know I just wanted a best friend — someone to fill the void inside?

This same pattern repeated itself into college.

When I graduated from high school, I moved from my home in Northern California to attend college in Southern California. I didn't own a car, so my first weeks were lonely. I was surprised to find out that someone I knew from home, Mark, lived in my dorm.

"You like football?" Mark asked.

Not really, but I didn't tell him that.

"A bunch of us guys watch Monday night football together and then have a Bible study afterward, if you wanna come sometime." He told me how he'd rededicated his life to Christ in the last year.

"Cool." I was looking for a place to connect; since I was raised Catholic, this seemed as good as any.

I enjoyed going to Bible study and hanging out with the guys, but I wanted something with more substance. When I asked Mark, he said the Monday night study was geared to new believers or "seekers."

"So you have another Bible study?" I asked.

Mark told me about Thursday nights. "We do a more in-depth study then. It's the same chapter in the Bible we study on Monday, but we delve deeper."

I couldn't wait to join.

"I gotta be honest about my struggles with porn," Rick told the group on the first Thursday night I attended. "I know I shouldn't buy the magazines, but it's like I'm addicted."

Rick was so vulnerable in front of everyone; I couldn't help but be impressed.

"I see a beautiful woman, and next thing I know, I'm undressing her in my mind," Rick admitted.

Several guys nodded in understanding.

We prayed for one another and then got into studying the Bible.

I don't know what I expected, but Thursday's group was a mix of ordinary guys, struggling with real problems, living out real faith. I'd never seen that before. My own family brushed our problems under the rug.

The more I studied the book of John, the more I saw my own inconsistencies. I saw my self-righteousness and my belief that I was above reproach. Wasn't I good enough? Didn't it count that I went to Mass every week? I didn't understand I needed a personal relationship with Jesus, so I decided to ask him into my heart.

Week after week, Rick was honest about the battle he faced with pornography. He asked for prayer and didn't pretend to have it all together. Other guys shared their struggles, too. It was my first glimpse into what healthy intimacy looked like.

I decided to open up to Rick about my homosexual tendencies, but I feared what he'd think. My emotions assaulted me, breaking me to the point of tears the night of Bible study.

"Dude, you okay?" My roommate looked at me like I'd gone off the deep end. "Girl problems?"

I left, brushing him off. I had to talk to Rick.

"Hey, Rick," I cleared my throat after the study finished.

"What's up?"

"Mind if we talk?" My voice squeaked.

Rick seemed to sense my need for privacy. "Want to take a walk?"

We didn't make it much farther than the dorm parking lot, but my courage didn't come for another 30 minutes.

"I kinda got this problem," I finally blurted out.

Rick was patient.

I exhaled. "You know how you struggle with porn?"

Rick kicked a pebble. "It's a daily battle, man."

RECOVERING MY MANHOOD

I choked up. "I struggle with my feelings about other guys."

There it was, out in the open. My awful secret.

But Rick didn't freak out like I'd imagined. "Mind if I tell some of the guys so we can pray for you?"

"No," I rushed. "You can't tell anyone."

Why'd I have to open my big mouth? I couldn't believe I'd actually shared my darkest secret, yet despite the shame that tore me up inside, I felt like I'd made a breakthrough.

"It took a lot of courage for you to tell me this." Rick put his arm on my shoulder. "I won't tell anyone till you're ready. In the meantime, I'll pray for you, Joe."

I continued to let others define my identity. My friends at Bible study accepted me, even if was too clingy. I tried to build healthy relationships, but something still eluded me.

"We need to talk," I confronted my parents. I'd be leaving soon for a semester abroad, so I wanted to be honest with my parents about what I was going through before I left.

My parents sat next to each other on the bed.

"I struggle with homosexual desires."

My parents eyed one another, but neither said anything negative.

"Whatever makes you happy, Joe," Mom smiled. "We won't judge you."

"You know what we believe, but we still just want you to be happy," my dad echoed.

SUFFICIENT TO **STAND**

The conversation left me infuriated. I wanted them to realize how I was trying to follow God and surrender my life, even this struggle, to him. I didn't want to hear them condone the very sin I was trying to turn from. Even worse, we never broached the subject again. My little secret was one more family issue to sweep under the carpet.

My time abroad refreshed me. Because of the language and cultural barriers, I didn't put high expectations on making deep, intimate relationships. I didn't pressure my friends to meet my every need; instead, we just hung out, and that was enough.

When I came back to the States, I decided to serve for a year with the Navigators, a ministry dedicated to encouraging people, one-on-one, to study the Bible, develop a deepening prayer life and memorize and apply scripture.

I knew I needed to confess my homosexual struggle to Paul, a Navigator who'd discipled me for two years.

"This feels bigger than me," Paul told me. "Maybe you should see a counselor."

Counseling? I couldn't believe his response. I felt like a freak.

I was hurt, but the more I thought about Paul's suggestion, the more I decided maybe he was right. Unfortunately, I couldn't afford much counseling, and the few I visited were the human equivalent of a washcloth — not the macho men I wanted to affirm my own masculinity.

When I moved to Texas with the Navigators, however, I connected with a Navigator counselor named Jack. He was a tough Vietnam vet with a heart for Jesus.

RECOVERING MY MANHOOD

"Your desires are good, but they are misdirected," Jack explained to me one day. "The object of your desires just needs adjusting." I chewed on that for a while. He continued to explain, "You want affirmation, but you're seeking it from man — not from God, your creator. No man or woman will ever fulfill the emptiness inside you. Christ alone will do that."

Another breakthrough.

I returned home to Northern California when my year with the Navigators was finished and ended up working for an insurance company.

"I hate my job," I groaned one day to a friend.

"You should join the Army with me!" Peter suggested. He was a man's man who wanted to become an Airborne Ranger. I shook my head. I wasn't enlisting. The Army was the last place I wanted to go.

"No, thank you."

Funny how God has a way of changing our hearts. The more I prayed about my future, the more I saw God pointing toward the Army. I found a job in the Army that seemed to fit what I wouldn't mind doing and also paid a really high bonus. Moreover, God seemed to nudge me to join the Army to challenge me to grow as a man.

Within a month, I had enlisted for five years.

Trouble came five days later. During my in-processing security check, I was asked if I'd ever seen a counselor.

When my answer was affirmative, it came out what I went to counseling for and my assignment was changed from my dream job to something I had always hated. I couldn't believe the twist my life had taken.

Is this some kind of cruel joke, God? Or did I hear you wrong?

Nine weeks couldn't have lasted longer.

Fortunately, I never needed to do the job the Army chose for me. Instead, my unit deployed to Iraq, and I was able to move into a staff position.

Life in Iraq was confining, like living in a concentration camp. I hated being stuck inside the compound with my weapon. I longed for the freedom to hike in the hills that surrounded us. I felt trapped and spiritually dry, but God challenged me to lead a Bible study. Though our group was small, I was able to disciple some fellow soldiers.

Jim was one. He and I connected at the motor pool because my vehicle was always breaking down, and he was a mechanic. Jim told me his wife had cheated on him, and they were getting a divorce, so I invited him to Bible study. Jim came, but he didn't feel comfortable praying in front of our small group.

"Prayer is just like talking to your best friend," I coached him, one-on-one, just like I'd been taught on staff with the Navigators.

"I don't know," Jim hesitated. "I'm not much of a talker."

"Try it," I challenged him.

"Right here?" His eyes betrayed fear. "In front of everyone?"

We weren't exactly in front of everyone, but we didn't

have a lot of privacy, either — one of the costs of war. "We could use a bunker."

Over the course of several months, I taught Joel how to pray and spend daily time reading and memorizing God's word.

Another soldier and I spent hours hanging out together, playing video games and watching movies. Since we shared the same living quarters, we spent many late nights talking about the issues he faced. I encouraged him that God is faithful.

"It's a boy," he burst into our tent one day. "I have a son!" A huge grin stretched across his face.

I slapped him on the back. "Congratulations, man."

"You gotta see my kid." He showed me pictures online.

Seeing the baby on the screen gave me a new appreciation for the sacrifice many of my buddies made for our country.

"I just wish I could hold the little guy," he teared up. "It's killing me inside to be away from him and my wife."

I could only imagine.

Even though my job was relatively "cushy," living under the constant stress of attack gave me new confidence in my masculinity. Staring fear in the face emboldened me.

The experience also bridged the differences between my father and I in a way I hadn't expected. Since my father had been drafted during Vietnam, we bonded in a new way. It was one of the rare times I knew my dad was proud of me.

As soon as I returned to my duty station in Alaska, I attended Friends Church in Fairbanks. I'd only been to this church once before my deployment when a friend invited me, but I'd thought about Friends Church many times in Iraq, and I couldn't wait to return.

Knowing my own struggles with homosexuality, I appreciated Pastor Wall's emphasis on God's grace. His transparency about his own walk of faith was unpretentious and refreshing. We're all sinners, Pastor reminded us. We all fall, and God's grace alone is what transforms us.

I know this grace more than many.

After my return from Iraq, when I fell into my temptation with Danny, I couldn't believe what I was doing. After just one week, I couldn't stand it any longer. I felt emptier than before — which in some ways elated me. Homosexuality no longer held a stronghold in my life.

"Did you like the movie?" Danny asked after we'd left the theater.

"Yeah," I nodded. I needed to break things off with Danny, so I suggested we drive around.

"There's something I need to tell you," I began.

Danny was inquisitive.

"I like you as a friend, but I can't mess around like this anymore," I told him. "It's wrong, and I even feel physically sick afterwards."

Danny's response surprised me. "That's cool."

We drove around post for a while, talking.

RECOVERING MY MANHOOD

"I feel like you understand me," Danny confided. "That hasn't happened much in my life."

I knew that longing to be understood all too well. But I knew someone who understood me more than anyone. His name was Jesus, and he waited for me with his arms outstretched.

I told Danny goodbye and walked toward my room. The brilliant colors of the sunset seemed to permeate my spirit, touching me with rays of orange and purple. An overwhelming sense of love washed over me. For the first time, I really saw myself as God saw me — a sinner in need of a Savior. All sin is equal in his eyes. God saw me at my worst, and yet, he still loves me.

God continues to work in my life. He's taken away the power my fantasy life held over me, and he's challenging me to gain confidence in underdeveloped areas in my life, such as sports. I've tried several things I'd never done before — competitive swimming, skiing and racquetball — and found that I really enjoy participating in these sports.

When I meet new friends, I no longer look for someone who can meet all my needs. Rather, I enjoy hanging out just to hang out. I especially enjoy being involved in a men's group through Friends Church and a community-based Bible study that meets once a week.

One of the friends I made is newly married, so I look to him as a model for what a new husband should do. He's patient when I ask him questions about handling finances and managing a home. I want to be the husband God wants me to be if he blesses me with a wife someday.

SUFFICIENT TO **STAND**

God has been opening me to minister to men who struggle with the same issues I face. Though a part of me wants to forget my past, I want God to use me in whatever way he sees fit — whatever that means.

Isaiah 42:16 says, "I will lead the blind by ways they have not known, along unfamiliar paths I will guide them; I will turn the darkness into light before them and make the rough places smooth. These are the things I will do; I will not forsake them."

I am the blind man, yet God leads me along these unfamiliar paths to recover my manhood. He's making the dark places light and the rough places smooth. Through it all, my God will never forsake me.

UNDER HIS THUMB
THE STORY OF ROBERT YAEGER
WRITTEN BY SANDRA EASTMAN

When the Stryker Brigade arrived in Iraq, it was during the hottest part of the summer. After the winter rains, and when spring was finally in sight, the temperatures of 80 and 90 degrees were a prize worth snatching, and we reveled in the feeling of home.

Water balloons flew between tents and laughter was coupled with the prattle of voices stretched across the camp. I had *borrowed* some wood from some Navy Seabees, determined to build us a nice deck to sit outside so we could relax and avoid the moon dust that followed after the winter rains.

I stood by my tent, the hammer slung over my shoulder, talking and laughing, while two of my friends were watching a movie. In a single moment — like a stealthy lion pouncing on his prey — the gigantic 122-millimeter rocket loomed across the atmosphere. *Boom!* For an instant, there was a deafening silence, then only blackness as we heard the whistling whine of the other rockets that followed.

***

I was born into the Army. From the time I was young, my dream was to have a career in the military. I even played soldier as a child. Being a member of our country's greatest lifetime occupation, the military, was part of my heritage. My great-grandfather's brother fought and died at the Battle of the Bulge during World War II, my own great-uncle fought in the Korean War, my grandfather fought in the Vietnam War and my father served in Operation Desert Storm. It seemed only right that I follow in their footsteps.

During the early part of my childhood, we traveled all over the country, never living in one spot for more than three years. When I was in the sixth grade, my father retired from the Army, and my family settled in Fort Worth, Texas. My two sisters weren't about to carry on the family heritage, so it was up to me. I approached my dad when I was in high school.

"I've decided to sign up for the Army's split option plan. I'll actually go to boot camp before I finish high school."

"I'm proud of you, son." My dad always encouraged me and sometimes my mom worried, but I guess that's what moms do.

I took my Basic Training at Fort Jackson in South Carolina. Then I decided to become a medic and was sent to Fort Sam Houston for training. I was 17 years old and officially in the Army. My life-long ambition was finally coming to fruition.

I was a medium-height, skinny kid with brown eyes and brown hair. I didn't really look like much of a soldier at my age and weight, but after training, I was ready to go where my country needed me.

UNDER HIS THUMB

In the summer of 2005, I was 20 years old, and I received my orders for Iraq. A few weeks before I left for Iraq, I bought a plastic card that displayed all the verses about putting on the armor of God. I brought it with me and always made sure to carry it.

Breaking Into a Different World

The average temperature in Iraq ranges from 120 degrees Fahrenheit in August to below freezing in January. Along with the temperature changes, there is the wind and the dust, the rain and the never-ending humidity.

We arrived in Iraq in August 2005, and were assigned to Combat Outpost Rawah in the Al Anbar province near the western Euphrates River Valley. We were to assist in the setup of a permanent combat outpost as part of an effort involving Army, Marine, Air Force and Special Operations Forces to prevent what was believed to be a strong presence of foreign terrorists from crossing the Syrian border into Iraq.

Rawah sat in a strategic location, with numerous roads passing by and a major highway from Syria in the east to Baghdad in the west. We were assigned to scout out the insurgents as they infiltrated from Syria.

The outpost was about the size of a small airport and had a helicopter pad, along with tents, but no amenities like running water or toilets. Not only was it far from a first-class hotel, it wasn't even a good campground. There was barbed wire around the perimeter and 8-foot HESCO

SUFFICIENT TO **STAND**

barriers around the tents for protection. The wire mesh containers, lined with plastic and filled with dirt, provided our only protection from the outside.

In the summer, we barely stepped outside our tents without dust flying in our faces. Sometimes it felt as if someone had turned on a hot blow dryer square into my face, while they were pouring sand over my head. We called it moon dust, that strange phenomena that mounded as much as 18 inches in spots and was so finely grained, it was almost like talcum powder sprinkled on a soft inland beach. I felt certain the winter had to be better, but again, I was wrong.

The winter brought so much rain it seemed as if God was trying to wash away all the remnants of death and destruction, but it was actually the typical weather for Iraq. I couldn't understand how a land supposedly at the heart of the world's creation could bring forth a climate that was barely for the living. The moon dust of summer was replaced by wet dirt the consistency of chocolate pudding. Even when we thought it was safe to step on it — *splat!* — we found ourselves boot deep or more in mud that wasn't easily removed.

Every day before I left to perform scout patrol, I prayed the Lord's Prayer faithfully. I knew if I were to return from Iraq, it would be because of God's help. As the days and weeks passed, I learned to cope with the heat and the rain, but I was always conscious of the danger that was all around me. I had heard the stories of men being blown to pieces in a single instant, and that was my greatest fear.

UNDER HIS THUMB

I didn't want to experience the devastating effects modern weapons can inflict on the human body. Every night, I felt the lonely desolation of war.

In December, I left my scout platoon to return to work in the aid station. I relaxed my guard and became somewhat complacent about my assignment. I didn't know the greatest test of all was going to come when I least expected it.

The MASH Team of Iraq

When a soldier is injured in war, the first person on the scene is the medic. He literally puts his own life at risk to determine the needs of the wounded soldier and then transport him or her back to a more stable and protected environment. Our unit worked just like the *MASH* TV show. There were two doctors working along with the rest of us. We had a strange yet forceful camaraderie that nothing could trample. We were there to piece our fellow soldiers back together. Being in the Army is like living in a huge house with 100 brothers; they tease you, they bully you, they have fun with you, but when the chips are down, they've got your back.

It was March 21, 2006, and we were all celebrating the end of winter with one of the first few warm days of spring. We knew the scorching sun and winds of summer would soon be upon us with temperatures in the 100s instead of the mild 80s we enjoyed that day. The guys decided it would be a great spring cleaning day. Most of us were running around in just our fatigues and no shirts, throwing water balloons, sparring with one another and having a good time.

Then — it happened.

From a 17-mile journey, the 122-millimeter rocket torpedoed into the camp and straight through the top of my tent.

My friends were catapulted off their bunks as everything went black. I could hear a high-pitched shrieking as the second and third rockets streaked across the camp and hit the outside wall.

As the blackness cleared, I saw a tiny pinhole of light gradually expanding itself as my eyes began to focus on the scene around me. The only sound I could hear was the ringing in my ears. Trembling, I stared in shock at the tent that had disintegrated around me and the soldier trembling on the ground below my feet.

He was attempting to low crawl away from the destruction, but only his arms and legs were flailing hopelessly in the air.

"Hey, buddy, I've got your back."

I picked him up by his shirt and dragged him over to the protective wall.

Shrapnel flew through the air, circling my body as if I were shielded with armor, and obliterated a nearby truck. It was so full of shrapnel, it looked like a colander.

Then my tent was ablaze with the orange and scarlet hues of fire.

Two soldiers rushed in and pulled out their dazed

brothers. Chaos flooded the campground as everyone frantically searched through the tents for the wounded. As I was the last one nearest to the explosion, they thought for sure I'd been hit, and I heard my fellow soldiers' panicked voices ringing through the camp.

"Yaeger! Yaeger, where are you?"

"I'm good, man," I hollered back to let them know I was okay. I was in shock that I was still standing.

I squeezed through a hole in one end of the tent to find my buddy, Barin. I panicked when I saw the stream of red fluid oozing down the inside wall.

"Barin, where are you, man?" I screamed.

My brothers sprinted up from behind me, and we all searched frantically through the shattered tent. Then one of the guys started to laugh. "Look, man. This is Kool-Aid! Not blood!" A large container of liquid had been shattered in the blast.

I ran my fingers nervously through my hair in sheer relief.

Barin had left the tent to serve guard duty. He was one lucky guy, or so we thought at the time.

When the dust started to clear, soldiers were seen hugging one another; some guys were crying, and some were vomiting just from the stress of the moment.

It was then I felt the pain in my back. Somewhere in the course of events, shrapnel about the size of a pencil eraser had found its way into my back. I glanced around at the camp and stood in amazement. We had four buildings, two trailers and numerous tents; all of them had been hit.

SUFFICIENT TO **STAND**

Everything in my tent was melted or riddled with debris. At that moment, I realized we had all just witnessed God's protection at work.

The 122-millimeter rocket was designed to kill everything within a 100-yard radius. By design, it should have killed most of us. We should have all been lying in body bags or on morgue slabs that day, but we weren't. One of the HESCO barriers was destroyed, but miraculously, no one in our camp died. The two soldiers that were blown from the tent only received slight concussions. The brigade surgeon that was visiting pulled the metal out of my back with a metal clamp, and I was again ready for combat.

The following day, we were instructed to replace the tent in the exact same location. We did as we were ordered, but after it was complete, no one would sleep in it. We all managed to find other places to sleep — outside, in a jeep, in another building. It didn't matter. No one was returning to that tent.

The Soldier's Psalm

Our regular chaplain was out of camp at this time, but his replacement came down to our tent to visit us. He sat us down and opened his Bible.

"You guys have been through a traumatic experience. I know you're all thankful to be alive. Now the Bible has a few things to say about God's protection, and I'd like to read you something from the 91st Psalm."

UNDER HIS THUMB

The wind graced his cheeks as he began to read the verses: "He that dwelleth in the secret place of the most high shall abide under the shadow of the Almighty. I will say of the Lord, he is refuge and my fortress, my God, in him will I trust. Surely he shall deliver thee from the snare of the fowler and the deadly pestilence. He shall cover thee with his feathers ... Because thou hast made the Lord which is my refuge, even the Most High my habitation. There shall be no evil befall thee, nor shall any plague come near thy dwelling. For he shall give his angels charge over thee, to keep thee in all thy ways."

None of us could believe this was actually in the Bible because it seemed to be written just for us. God was giving us his promise; no evil should befall us. So the next night, we all slept in the tent.

When our regular chaplain returned, I told him how I was feeling. "I really know God protected and had his hand on me, especially. I know I want to trust in him completely for my life."

"Robert, there are several others who have expressed their faith to me and asked to be baptized. Would you like to be one of them?"

I nodded. "I'd like that very much."

Three weeks after the explosion, a group of us traveled to the Euphrates River. It was a fearful journey that took a lot of prayer just to commence. The area had hardly been patrolled, and we had to leave our weapons in the truck and wade into the river unarmed. I felt so vulnerable; I had to trust in God to watch over and protect me. I felt like I was on this dangerous mission just to be able to profess my faith.

As I sank down into the water, a cool, fresh feeling overwhelmed me, and I knew I had found my own personal faith in God, and no matter what happened in the months to come, God would be with me for the good and the bad.

Over the next six months, our unit suffered several casualties, but I never doubted God and his plan for me. I knew he was in control, and I never found myself angry at him. I just kept remembering how he spared my life, and I was confident he had a greater purpose for me. I had married before leaving for Iraq, but after the rocket incident, my wife decided to divorce me. I knew other guys that were going through the same ordeal, but somehow, even through that pain, I still trusted in God's plan for me.

In July, we were scheduled to return home. Just 12 hours before departure, the Department of Defense announced our stay in Iraq was to be extended for four more months and we would be transferred to Baghdad. Everyone was immediately devastated, but eventually, we accepted the fact that we couldn't change our destiny. No one knew the worst was yet to come.

The Lights of Baghdad

The glistening lights of Baghdad give a false sense of welcome that is diminished by the illumination of guided missiles providing their own spectacular light show. The missiles replace the hope of a glittering world with death and destruction. Sewage fills the streets as there is no established infrastructure to accommodate everyday living.

The first few days of our arrival in Baghdad were spent in a pity party that was short-lived. It didn't take long before everyone stepped up to the plate and joined in the game. We all did our jobs and quickly adapted to our new routine.

I was given the job of senior medic in charge of the medical care of about 100 men. We had to actually go out on the scout patrols and were usually the first to approach soldiers wounded in battle. A lot of our time was also spent patrolling the city and trying to motivate the people to help their country and fight the insurgents. It was a constant uphill battle. Seeing the death all around me and being unable to prevent it was one of the toughest things I'd ever faced.

We were the first part of the surge to end the war — 4,000 soldiers executing a job that required 20,000.

Going Home

On November 25, 2006, the first wave of Stryker soldiers returned to Fairbanks, Alaska, after serving 16 months in Iraq. It was 32 degrees below zero at Fort Wainwright on Saturday morning — a 102-degree difference from Baghdad.

As I stepped off the bus that transported us from the local Air Force base to our home at Fort Wainwright, I was overwhelmed by strings of shouting and crying families waving homemade banners and bearing bright balloons as the Army band played patriotic tunes in the corner.

I watched as wives sprinted across the Alert Holding Area into the arms of soldiers, who were smiling, bawling and showing emotion like they hadn't been able to for a year and a half. I saw children leap into the arms of fathers, girlfriends leap into the arms of young privates. Joy seemed to just emanate from the room.

It should have been a happy occasion, a celebration to a long 16 months that had rattled my body and shaken my existence. Instead, it was an ironic reminder that I had no one there to celebrate with; my parents lived in Texas, and my wife had divorced me. And I wasn't the only one.

About two-thirds of the soldiers arriving in Fairbanks had no one waiting to greet them. The rumor in the Army is that the stress of war is responsible for seven out of 10 marriages ending in divorce.

Thankfully, my friends didn't let me bask in that lonely moment; a buddy invited me to spend time with him and his wife and their children.

At Christmas, I visited my parents, and my mom broke down the minute she saw me.

"Thank God you made it back," she cried.

I had called her after the rocket incident to tell her I was okay, and she had worried every day since.

"God was watching over me, Mom, and that's the reason I'm here today."

UNDER HIS THUMB

It was a wonderful holiday and sure beat the previous Christmas I spent in Iraq. My mom wept when I gave her the Purple Heart I received after the rocket attack.

Not long after I arrived back at Fort Wainwright, a friend invited me to dinner. It was then I met Tracy, who has since become the one woman in my life. She is a wonderful Christian girl who is also in the Army and is stationed 100 miles from me. We are still able to spend four out of 10 days together, hold a Bible study and share devotions together. I never realized how meaningful a relationship could be when God is part of the combination.

I may have to return to Iraq next year, but I am still waiting on that order. I have decided to switch my profession from a medic to a special investigator. If that change is approved, perhaps I will not have to return. I feel a little bit like I'm sitting on the bench right now while my team is playing in the game. Hearing about the war on television or reading the newspaper and knowing they are there fighting without me is hard. Sometimes I have the urge to get back in the game, if for nothing else but to be out there for my team.

When I arrived home, I experienced the typical nightmares, but they have subsided into a fear that causes me to jump at any noise that sounds like rockets or gunfire.

One night, Tracy was staying with me and locals were celebrating a Cinco de Mayo party a few streets away. I was sleeping when a large rocket popped outside our window. Tracy ran to see what had happened, but I took a different course of action.

SUFFICIENT TO **STAND**

"Get down, get down!" I hollered.

Stunned, she turned from the window.

"Don't you ever do that again!" I quickly reprimanded her. "Next time that happens, you get down on the ground or you'll get hurt."

The next morning, Tracy smiled at me over breakfast.

"So, you were very busy last night trying to teach me how to be a soldier."

We laughed together about the episode. I guess it takes a long time to get over it all, and it's just something I'll have to work through.

The other day, I was watching a television program where a Vietnam veteran was interviewing a 96-year-old soldier who fought in World War I.

"So, did you have a lot of nightmares when you returned from the war?" the Nam vet asked.

The old soldier nodded and replied, "They never seem to leave you."

"So, it's been more than 50 years for you; when did you have your last nightmare?"

The older man smiled a little and his eyes glossed over.

"It was last night," he replied.

That statement alone reveals a lot about war. I feel good about what we accomplished in Iraq and about what we're doing. The people over there don't hate Christians like the stories in the American media often portray. The Iraqi soldiers are glad we're there to help them, as there's not much patriotism among the people of Iraq. The children love us. When we wear our sunglasses and offer them

70

UNDER HIS THUMB

candy, they think we are American movie stars. The children in Iraq are special people. One day, I gave a small mentally challenged boy a couple of suckers. Instead of eating them himself, he promptly found two soldiers and gave them away.

As far as my own experience in Iraq, I now carry in my heart the 91st Psalm and remember well the verses. The Hebrew translation actually reads, "He (God) shall defend me under his feathered wings, and under his overspreading wings shalt you flee for protection. His trustworthiness shall be your shield and he will surround you with a fence for your protection."

None of us will ever forget that day in March when God lovingly spread his arms out to protect us. Everyone in our camp had to admit that something very special happened that day, and the chapel suddenly became very crowded on Sundays.

Of course, some of the guys just laughed it off, but one of my friends, who was standing close to the tent with me, put it this way, "God had his hand over that tent and his thumb over us."

The 122-millimeter rocket should have destroyed our camp and killed many people, but not one soldier died. I know in my heart God was the most important player in the game that day. Now I am confident I no longer have to worry about tomorrow, because I am certain God knows the future. I can live each day trusting that he is doing his best for me, because I know one thing for certain — he's got my back.

FOR YOUR EYES ONLY
THE STORY OF NATHAN COHOON
WRITTEN BY BETH ROTEN

"Oh, gross!" I shouted, slamming the magazine shut.

"Shut up," Robby retorted. "My mom will hear, and we'll be in trouble."

"Oh, man." I shook my head as images of nude adults imprinted themselves on my first-grade mind. I snuck another peek, giggling at the way the models posed.

Robby was giggling, too, when his parents' bedroom door swung open. There stood his mom, and boy was she mad!

"What are you two doing?" she demanded. As if she didn't already know.

I gulped. Robby looked up shamefully with beads of sweat glistening on his forehead. All of a sudden, the spacious master bedroom, with its canopy bed and safari décor, shrunk down to the size of a jail cell. All I could do was sit there, staring at the floor.

"Get up from there right now." She was beet red. I didn't realize it at the time, but she was probably as mortified and embarrassed as we were. Robby and I found the magazines in the master bedroom closet, where his father had so stealthily hidden them.

We both rose slowly to our feet, depositing the magazines on the bed. With heads still bowed, we trudged out of the room, down the hall and downstairs.

Robby's mom slammed the bedroom door shut and

SUFFICIENT TO **STAND**

followed us down the stairs, her aqua eyes boring holes in our backs. When we reached the kitchen, she ordered us outside.

"I want you to stay outside and play," my friend's mom yelled as she trailed after us. "No more being upstairs since I can't trust you to behave." We stopped at the door and looked up at her sheepishly. She ran her long fingers through her jet-black hair and sighed. "You two …" Then she shook her head and walked back into the house.

Once we reached the safety of the backyard, Robby and I looked at each other. Finally free of condemning eyes, we burst out laughing and ran for the park, just down the street from Robby's house. Soon, our minds were on the business of play, and I thought nothing else of the images I'd seen that day.

However, those images were permanently branded on my mind. Neither Robby nor I grasped the spiritual impact this one episode would make on our lives until much later.

In junior high and high school, my friends and I traveled to the local bookstore to sneak a peek at pornographic material whenever we got the chance. I would think, *Wow! Oh, man! I like this feeling even though I really don't understand it.* Eventually, we'd get kicked out for being minors.

I didn't let anyone know what I was doing. I knew if my parents or my siblings ever found out, I'd be dead. If my friends found out, all my talk about church and God for all those years would make me look like a fool. If kids

FOR YOUR EYES ONLY

would tell dirty jokes at school, my comment would usually be, "That's awful." Yet, whenever I was alone, there was this rabid hunger to see the images over and over again. The thought never occurred to me that I was descending into a pit of shame.

At age 18, I was excited to be able to hang out at a strip club. I walked in alone and sat at a small table near the platform where the exotic dancers shook their bodies and deposited their clothing on the stage. I watched, completely entranced. I left there with a new thrill, one that magazines wouldn't fill anymore. Only when I couldn't make it to a strip club would magazines fill my desire.

At age 19, I joined the Army. Bamberg, Germany, was the first place I was stationed. The military was good for me, and my life started to fall into place. I enjoyed what I was doing on the job, but I still made time for my secret obsession. Still, if the guys would tell dirty jokes or attend R-rated movies, I would decline to participate, saying, "No, I don't like it. I shouldn't be involved in that stuff."

I was an honest-to-goodness hypocrite. No matter what I didn't do with the crowd, what I was doing at home alone was making me feel worse and worse inside. Every image I viewed made me feel excited one moment and disgusted at myself the next. I was spiraling downward, deeper and deeper into shame.

The reason for that growing emptiness is probably because all my childhood, I attended church. God was real to me from an early age. My parents read us Bible stories, and we all tried to live Christian lives in every aspect.

SUFFICIENT TO **STAND**

That's why by the time I was grown, I knew I could never let anyone in my family know my secret.

It wasn't until I was about 23 years old that I began to seriously evaluate my walk with Christ, or lack thereof. I began to pray and connect with God. It was then God revealed to me the path I was on and the result of continuing down that path, if that's what I chose to do. But he also showed me how the path of my pornography obsession began. I realized Satan hooked me on his fishing rod with that first peek at Playboy so long ago. Then he very, very patiently began reeling in his line over all those years.

This trap I am in … it was laid for me all the way back in the first grade! Satan is patient. He just keeps feeding me the junk, and I keep taking the bait.

By this time, I was stationed at Fort Riley, Kansas. It was there I met a wonderful group of brothers and sisters called Cats for Christ, a college ministry with Kansas State in Manhattan, Kansas. There I received an abundance of support and love.

I decided to join a Bible study group called Josiah's Priests with the brothers of Cats for Christ. We met weekly and studied out of a popular book that discussed every man's battle with remaining pure. I wanted to have a clear head again. I knew what I was doing was wrong; I just needed someone to help direct me in the right way to think.

I was only in the group for two weeks before being shipped to Fort Richardson, Alaska. When I arrived, I had no idea how many learning experiences were in store for

FOR YOUR EYES ONLY

me. I started completing the lessons and reading the book on my own. I learned how to start "bouncing" my eyes off women in general, but also how to look in their eyes when I talked to them. I never realized how obvious it was that I was checking them out and that I really wasn't being stealthy.

Up until this point, I had not really given Bible study a high priority in my life, although I occasionally read a scripture here and there. One Wednesday evening, I was at church service when Pastor Smith told us the method that he used to keep himself in the word of God. He said each morning he read a chapter out of the Old Testament and one out of the New Testament, along with the Proverbs of the day. I took his advice and began to implement his idea into my own daily routine. After PT, when we were released for hygiene and chow, I would sit in my office and read using Pastor Smith's technique. I liked starting my day by thinking about God's word, and it helped keep me focused on God's plan for my life that day.

While at Fort Richardson, I was able to make some great friends through a class that focused around college and career-type single people. It was really good to spend time with other Christians after dealing with work and negative influences all day. Eventually, I met a wonderful and very beautiful woman who knocked me right out. We developed a real friendship, and after much prayer, I worked up the nerve to ask her on a date. Talk about feeling like a kid again! I was 25 years old and experienced shaky knees and red-faced shyness all over again.

77

SUFFICIENT TO **STAND**

We started dating, and all the while, I knew I would have to come clean with her about my "mask" if we were to have a true and honest relationship. I finally told her, and it hurt her very much. I knew she never had any idea that I dealt with this sort of problem; after all, I was the master of disguise. Our relationship did not end because of it, but it definitely posed some serious discussions about where my life was heading. Her father was concerned about it and was not happy I lied to his daughter about my true self. Things continued to go downhill between her father and I, but my mind shifted to my impending deployment to Iraq.

In Iraq, the pendulum of temperature swung to the other extreme. The heat was oppressive. It is not unusual to experience temperatures exceeding 120 degrees Fahrenheit, but we set up fans and air conditioners to help keep our rooms cool.

This was my second deployment, and what was supposed to have been a year-long tour turned out to be a 16-month stay. During the long hitch in Iraq, my thoughts continued to spiral downhill. Anxiety began to creep in like a snake slithering into a camper's sleeping bag, but I hid it well. I did talk to my battalion chaplain, and he provided good advice. Life in Iraq was still difficult, especially in my work environment. It seemed like I was the only one who made feeble attempts to not soak in pornography. Walking by someone looking at a magazine, I'd glance to see if it fed my "passion." I would sneak a peek at open computers if the owner stepped away. Just a few clicks, and there was the image the black hole inside me wanted to bask in.

Eventually, I started to crack down on my evil habit. I'd flip over magazines so they weren't visible or I'd stuff them in the trash can. I even went so far as to close other people's laptops so I wouldn't have to see the pictures.

When I arrived back in Alaska, it was the dead of winter. I took the month of January off and visited home. The stay there was okay, but I found myself focusing on work and the impending responsibility I would soon have as a platoon sergeant. It wouldn't be that hard of a job, but there would be tough times I knew I would have to overcome. Anxiety just kept building and building inside me.

When I returned to Fort Wainwright in February, the weather was as bad as my attitude. Seasonal Affect Disorder (SAD) is a very real condition. The lack of sunlight can cause some people to become extremely depressed. I didn't have a doctor diagnose me with SAD, but I sure felt the effects. The excessive darkness during the winter months didn't affect me for the first three years I was there, but the inner turmoil raging inside me did. By this time, Satan was driving me all over the road, and I was a wreck inside.

I drove up to the back gate for physical fitness every morning, since it was the shortest route, where I was met by a guard named Dewey. He bore the biggest smile I'd ever seen.

"Hello, brother," he called out from the guard shack, "how are ya today?"

"Miserable," I commented, showing him my identification.

"Well, you need to let God change that for you …
okay?" he nudged, smiling and waving me in.

I felt like an arrow had just hit me in the chest.
"Humph," I grunted, rolling up my window against the
below-zero temperature.

Day after day, I saw Dewey at the back gate when I
drove onto base to go to work. Every day, it seemed as
though his smile grew larger.

Now, even though I wasn't on the front lines and had
not even ventured beyond the safety of the protective wire
in Iraq, I was facing depression and anxiety on a horrible
level.

*What am I going to do? I'm so embarrassed to go to
my supervisor. What will he think of me? That I truly am
a hypocrite and a monster? Will he think I'm a wacko, not
fit for duty due to my depression?*

On top of all this, suicide became a real issue for me. I
never thought I could really go through with it, but Satan
was tempting me with a permanent solution to my temporary problems. This really frightened me and was what led
me to finally talk to my first sergeant.

The war of decision raged in me for a few weeks. Every
day, I had to encounter Dewey's genuine joy and know
mine had been forfeited. Every day, I had to see my supervisor and work up the courage to ask for help. Every day, I
had to look at myself in the mirror at the horrible mess I'd
become.

During this time, I began to attend services at the

FOR YOUR EYES ONLY

Church of God of Prophecy. Immediately, the church family surrounded me with love and acceptance, which made dealing with my secret even harder. But it was nice to know they were praying for me.

With my depression, anxiety, work and Satan constantly yelling at me just to commit suicide and get it over with, the situation started to reach beyond my ability to comprehend, much less deal with, on my own. I knew what I needed to do. As soon as I arrived at work, I located my first sergeant and told him everything.

Within a few days, I secured my appointment with the mental health doctor. The man smiled and looked at me for a long time before he introduced himself. "I'm Dr. Carter, and if you will let me, I'd like to help you."

"Okay," I replied guardedly.

He went on to tell me he was a Christian, too. How amazing God is, when he is working in our lives. I had prayed, "Lord, please let me see a Christian doctor, whoever it might be." And God gave me what I asked for.

The doctor asked, "How would you rate your stress level in Iraq?"

"I didn't have problems out there," I blurted out.

"Well," Dr. Carter began, still looking at me with a smile, "even though your stress level was low, there are still effects from just being there, behind the wire."

"I guess so," I mumbled.

That first visit led to another and another. I was hospitalized twice for the anxiety and depression, but the visits really made a huge difference. I learned from the doctors, nurses and hospital staff about how to manage my time, relax my body and pray to relieve mounting stress.

I told my girlfriend and her father what was going on. While I was in the hospital, I held a few very open and honest talks with her father. Truth and understanding came out on both sides, and although my girlfriend and I ended up breaking off the relationship, I am glad to say I call her dad a friend and fellow brother in Christ.

While I was in the hospital, I obviously had to inform my family of what was going on. I ended up confessing to my entire family, via e-mail, my addiction to pornography. After I left the hospital, I installed a Christian Internet filter on my computer, and my brother actually became my accountability partner and controlled the password to that filter.

When I eventually returned to work, Dewey stood at the gate again.

"Hello, brother," he began.

I interrupted with, "And hello back to you! How are you today?"

His usual smile grew even bigger. "God is good. God is good," he replied, waving me through.

The next morning, I awoke, uttering out loud, "Thank you, God, for this morning. You are great." I began to view each day differently. There was a possible adventure each day, if I could see it. That became a journey for me in itself. I pulled out my Bible and slowly began to understand rather than just listen to God's word. I also began applying what the Bible says in "writing the scripture on

FOR YOUR EYES ONLY

your heart." (Proverbs 3:1-4, 7:1-5)

I started memorizing verses to use on Satan when he tempted me, like Lamentations 3:21-23, Philippians 4:6-5 and 1 Peter 5:7. A friend advised and mentored me on learning Psalm 1 and James 1. Verses I heard as a child also started flowing back into my brain like a river of love and contentment.

I also learned my friend's wife experienced severe depression, and she shared her struggle with me. She told me whenever Satan tempted her, she would take authority in God's name. She would tell Satan these thoughts were not of God and that by the power of God through Jesus Christ, he was bound. I have used this in my own life, and when my heart is right with God, this works for me.

When I was released from the hospital, I decided to call each of my family members and talk to them individually about all that had been going on in my life. First, I called my brother. He was so understanding and willing to help hold me accountable. After that conversation, I stood in the middle of the living room where I had been pacing throughout the entire call. I pressed the button on the phone to make another call. This time, I would talk to my mom. Then, I called my dad. They had recently divorced. Then, I called my other siblings. Everyone was forgiving. Not one of them would have guessed I had a problem with porn. I was amazed. By the time I was done calling everyone, it was late, and time to go to bed.

I lay in my bed and prayed, "God, thank you for helping me admit to all this. It's been a long day."

SUFFICIENT TO **STAND**

Every time the temptation to sneak a peek at the computer arose, I would literally put my hand up to my head, "grab" the thought out of my mind and throw it away, at God's feet. That simple action made such a difference. I didn't even say anything out loud. I don't know if anyone at work ever saw me do that, but if they did, they never mentioned it.

Along with the accountability measures, I still see my psychiatrist about every two months. I still suffer bouts of anxiety and depression, but now I have the tools and means to call on God for help.

I do not struggle with pornography like I used to, even though the temptation is still there. I can be walking down the street and the temptation will jump out at me from the advertisements around town, or the window of a bookstore known to sell questionable magazines.

When the temptation hits, I take authority over it, and I remind Satan who has control of my life — God.

I read the Bible, study and pray more than ever. After having told my church family about my addiction, they have been supportive, loving and accepting. I couldn't ask for a better place to be.

I attend a weekly Bible study called The Hospitality House, which is run by missionaries who reach out to military personnel. We meet once a week for dinner and a Bible study where we ask questions, debate topics and use a step-by-step method in learning Bible truths. I do slack off at times, but like most people, I am a work in progress.

At the most terrible moments of temptation, I pray. I

put aside the worries, let God flood my heart and mind and listen for what he might speak to me. Usually, it's an impression to do or say something to someone to encourage him and get my mind off my own stress.

I have read the Bible off and on my whole life, but now things are simply jumping off the page at me. I have a pro-active faith; in everything I do or say, I try to let my actions, words and thoughts show I am a Christian without me having to tell someone straight out. I still struggle at times and I fail. But the Lord is there to pick me up and dust me off when I return my heart to Christ who forgives us and helps in "running the race." (1 Corinthians 9:24-27)

I have become more outspoken than I used to be, when the need arises. I can easily walk up to someone and say, "Hey, I'm a Christian, and this is what I believe." Not perfect at it, but I'm learning. I just try to let God lead me because now I am living my life for him.

THE TRUTH SHALL MAKE YOU FREE
THE STORY OF LAUREN
WRITTEN BY SANDRA EASTMAN

"You're not my dad! Do you think you can come into our home and pretend to take his place?"

Roy was about to speak but was interrupted.

"Lauren, calm down," my mother interjected. "Roy isn't trying to take your dad's place, but he did leave his family."

"That's not true," I snapped back at her while stamping my foot in righteous indignation. "You decided to get a divorce, and then you tried to back out. Now you're blaming Dad?"

"I will never forgive your father for leaving us, and I had to find a way to provide for my children."

Roy shook his head and walked from the room.

My mother scowled at me. "Now look what you've done."

"Well, you should have warned Roy that you only married him for his money. You know you don't even love him."

My mother threw me a sheepish grin. "That's not true."

"Ha! I can see it by the look on your face. You know what, Mom, you claim my dad was a terrible husband, but he was a wonderful father and still is."

SUFFICIENT TO **STAND**

"Well, Roy will be your father now."

I could feel my face flush red. "You've only known him for six months, and you not only marry him, but expect me to accept him as my dad? Don't count on it!"

***

Growing up in California garnered me a stable home life with two sisters, one brother and two parents, who I thought loved each other. I remember arriving home from school to the smell of fresh baked cookies and an immaculate house. Dinners were spent together as a family, and my parents worked hard at doing a good job of raising us. After my parents divorced, everything changed.

My world went from a clean, organized lifestyle to one of chaos and mess. My dad had been the catalyst that kept our life stable and structured — without him, it was gone.

Mom no longer cared about baking or cleaning. She went through the motions of providing a stable home, taking us to school activities and trying to be a good mom. It was so hard for my siblings and me to watch, but her anger and inability to forgive my father kept her from succeeding.

I was as independent then as I am now. After my father left, I abandoned our home, too, emotionally. I did everything I could to involve myself in activities that would keep me busy and away from home. I was so frustrated that Mom could never get over Dad leaving. We couldn't even be happy about a birthday or Christmas gift from Dad because Mom would act like a freak even hearing his name, let alone us being happy about something he did.

My uncle is a strong Christian, and I think that's what first spurred my interest in God. Mom and Dad didn't go to church much, but they would sometimes drive us to Sunday school and drop us off.

When my parents divorced, things seemed to change spiritually for my dad. He dedicated his life to God, and it was an amazing transformation. He went from not even attending church to praying about almost everything he did. Whenever there was a question or a decision to be made, my dad would say, "Let's pray about it."

We could see and feel Dad had changed as Christ just radiated from him. He worked very hard to lead each of us kids into a personal relationship with the Lord. As a teenager, I would visit Dad during the summer, and it was then I made a commitment to Christ that was meaningful in my life.

Somehow, I never felt any resentment toward my dad for the divorce. It was only the heartbreak of being apart from him that was so tough. All four of us siblings were so close and have remained so all our lives.

After high school, I left my mother and my home and moved to Fairbanks, Alaska, to live with my dad for two years. He worked on the north slope of Alaska for weeks at a time and then would be off work for weeks at a time. I found a job as a bank teller and moved into an apartment with a friend six months later. I still saw my dad on a regular basis, and our relationship remained strong.

At the time, my mother's pain over my departure seemed a moot point. I had to get away from her. She felt so justified in her anger, but it was only herself she was hurting. She just couldn't understand her resentment was pushing me farther away from her and closer toward my dad.

When I left Alaska, it was to housesit for a friend in Hawaii. I stopped in California to touch base with my family and high school friends. Once I was back home, I realized I missed my friends and family. So I decided not to return to Alaska.

I think part of the reason I was drawn to Bill was my dad had previously expressed his belief that I would some-day marry him. I'm not sure why my dad had this strange premonition. Bill wasn't someone I would normally con-sider dating, but his personality was very inviting.

He and I were buddies in high school and often at-tended events and activities within the same circle of friends. It was kind of like we both wondered if there could be something romantic between us, but neither of us ever pursued it.

Once I was back in California, the friendship Bill and I once knew blossomed into a romantic relationship, and we fell in love. Six months later, we were married. I was 19 years old. Our first child was born when I was 21 years old. The second and third child followed, each only 21 months apart. Two girls and one boy all under 5 years old were an overwhelming proposition for any young mother,

THE TRUTH

but it was devastating for one without any emotional support.

Bill was a real estate broker and developer, and his work brought a great deal of stress into our lives. What started out as a happy marriage soon began to crumble under the stress of responsibility. We were so young, and neither of us really had very good role models of what parents should be like. The emotional stress of Bill's job and the three kids at home were issues that we just didn't know how to deal with.

"I can't believe you have to take out another loan," I questioned. "I thought this deal was going to be the one that got us in the black."

"Look, Lauren. This is my business. You have to let me make the decisions."

"I can't stand not knowing where our next meal is coming from. We have three children to think about," I cried.

"I'm doing the best I can, Lauren. It doesn't help that I always hear you on the phone complaining about what a bad husband I am to your sisters."

I was sobbing by this time. "I have to talk to somebody, and my sisters will always listen."

"Well, maybe they need to listen to this: stay out of my business!"

After many, many similar arguments, Bill and I began spending less and less time together. As a result, I began to feel less loved, less wanted and more alone. I felt I was in an empty relationship, at home with my kids and had no life outside of that existence. I spent many days extremely depressed, and it seemed like no one even noticed.

Finally, I decided to quit planning a pity party for myself and do something positive. I loved my babies so much, but being in the house with them day and night left me exhausted. Sports had always been my outlet to escape my mom when I was a teenager, so I decided to join a softball league to try and regain some of my triumphant youth.

My softball coach was a charismatic man who made me feel special and important. One night, after a game, he offered to buy me coffee. He made no apologies for his behavior.

"Lauren, you're a beautiful woman, and I am very attracted to you. I sense you feel the same about me. If you'd be willing, we could spend a lot more time together."

I had a crush on the man since the season began, but just the fact that he noticed my intentions made me feel extremely uncomfortable.

What was I thinking?

I forced a smile. "I appreciate your honesty and the compliment, but I'm a married woman. I couldn't even begin to think about any relationship. I'm committed to my marriage."

And in my mind, I was very committed to my family; so much so that I wouldn't even consider a divorce or separation, no matter how broke we were or how depressed I became. Sometimes at night, I would fall into bed so spent from the stress of the day, my legs like rubber and my head pounding. Sometimes I just wanted to run away, but then I'd feel so guilty about even thinking such a thought. My children meant everything to me, and I refused to put them through a divorce like I suffered as a child.

By the time we entered our sixth year of marriage, we were living in a valley of distrust and alienation. We rarely spoke, and when we did, we argued, mostly about money and our future. We tried date nights, spending time one-on-one, but nothing seemed to matter.

We began to hang out with another couple who also had three children, and we enjoyed camping together. Bill would always flirt with Ellen, and she would reciprocate.

She appeared so starved for attention. I tried to ignore Bill's obvious fixation with Ellen, but it grated on me. Then Ellen and Jake put their house on the market. Of course, Bill stepped up to the plate and offered to help them with his exceptional real estate skills.

Our marriage problems continued, and we grew further apart. I was like an ostrich, my head firmly planted in the sand, not wishing to see the relationship between Bill and Ellen. One night, I even invited her to come along for girls' night out. I guess I thought if we could remain close friends, perhaps she'd stay away from my husband.

After the evening broke up, I came home to find Bill and Ellen sitting in her car outside my house. The kids were sleeping inside.

I walked up to the window and tapped lightly. "What's going on?" I asked when Bill rolled down the window.

"Aw, we're just discussing the house business," he re-

SUFFICIENT TO **STAND**

plied, bolting out of the car and hurrying toward the house.

I threw a questionable look at Ellen, and she invited me into the car. "Come on and drive with me, Lauren."

As we drove around, I tried to be as honest as I could with her. "Ellen, I know you and Jake are having a hard time in your marriage, and we are, too. Just please don't allow your marriage problems to involve my husband." My mind was screaming, *If you want to have an affair, don't have it with my husband!*

It wasn't long after that it seemed like Bill was deliberately causing arguments. Then he would pack his bags and walk out the door. I never knew the reason why, but I suspected he was spending time with Ellen. The first time it happened, my eyes were suddenly opened.

It was two days before our daughter's 2nd birthday. I didn't know what to do. I had no money to buy a gift for my little girl, so I called my sister and wept.

"I just don't know what to do anymore." I sniffed back tears.

"What's the matter with Bill? Doesn't he care about his kids anymore?" my sister replied.

"He — he's cheating on me. I'm sure of it," I sobbed. "I can't do this anymore. He just doesn't want to try."

After we hung up the phone, I wiped away my tears and looked in on the children. I was determined to make my daughter's birthday special for her in every way I could. I baked some cupcakes and found some candles. We sang happy birthday, and I took pictures. I refused to allow my pain and Bill's selfishness to spoil her day.

The kids and I spent the whole day making my daughter feel special. We didn't have fancy presents or expensive decorations, but that day, God showed me we didn't need any of those things. He made me feel his love would always be there for me as the only thing we would ever need. He taught me family is what matters most, and I knew I would never be alone again, no matter what was happening in my marriage.

That night, I sat alone, tears streaming down my cheeks. I brushed them away with my fingertips and swallowed hard. I stood up and reached for my Bible. As I searched the scriptures, trying to find an answer or something to lead me out of this horrible situation, it was as if someone blasted me in the face with a bright light. I could finally see what I had been missing. I always focused on what Bill could do to be a better husband and father, but I never thought about what I could do. I knew in my heart Bill had made some really bad choices, but that night, alone with God, I knew I had made some of the bad ones, too. That night, I prayed for God's forgiveness.

"Dear Lord, please forgive my own shortcomings and single sight. I've been so adamant about not getting divorced, I've forgotten to look at my own mistakes and what I could have done better in my marriage."

I knew God was finally telling me I was accountable, too. I knew it was possibly too late to save my marriage, but I made up my mind to let God make that decision.

We hadn't been attending church for some time, but

SUFFICIENT TO **STAND**

my decision to follow God's will was pointing me back there. I took my children and began to attend church again. I became involved in Bible studies and women's groups. I knew I needed the support of other Christians if I were to survive.

Bill came back again after that but only stayed a short time. The game continued with Bill leaving me for Ellen and then returning, feeling guilty about the affair. Ellen would play the martyr and tell him they had to return to their respective families for the children's sake. It was a very good ploy on her part, because Bill thought of her as a saint and couldn't stop loving her. He even admitted that the evening I caught them sitting in the car, they were planning a way to leave their respective spouses.

His interim return home was always filled with apathy and regrets about leaving Ellen. It ripped me up inside when he would tell me verbally how much he missed her when they were apart.

I'm not sure why I tolerated it, but I guess I was stuck in my own determination to save my marriage. I was blinded by my own strength of mind. At one point, we even considered moving to Oregon, just to save Bill the temptation of seeing Ellen. I always felt if Bill would just try and make some effort, we could revive our marriage. I never turned from God and knew he would help us if we would both open our hearts and ask for it. I just couldn't live with myself if I at least didn't try to do something.

In November of that year, Bill came home a few weeks before Thanksgiving, after being gone for a month. He

96

THE TRUTH

took the kids to see Santa at the mall the following day.

"Mommy, we had so much fun with her," my daughter giggled when they returned. "We saw Ellen at the mall, and she ate lunch with us."

I smiled through my tears. "That's great, honey. I'm so happy you had a good time."

I left the room in tears, but Bill didn't even apologize. The next day, he returned to Ellen and stayed with her until Christmas. The rollercoaster lasted almost a year when I finally insisted on counseling.

The pastor looked across the room at Bill. "So are you still involved in an affair?" He was pretty blunt with his questions.

"Oh, we just talk right now. We're not sleeping together," Bill grunted.

"Were you sleeping together?"

"Yes, but it was while we were separated."

I knew Bill and Ellen had been sleeping together for a long time. I could sense it by the way he treated me and how he acted, although I had never heard it before that day. The game of infidelity was difficult for a transparent human being.

I was sobbing as the two of them spoke, and the minister looked at me with sympathy in his eyes. He turned to Bill.

"I'm going to say this quite frankly, Bill. You can't have a wife and a girlfriend, too. You'd better decide which one you want."

My heart was pounding. I wanted so much for him to

SUFFICIENT TO **STAND**

pick me and the children.

As we left, the minister put his hand on Bill's shoulder. "I hope you make the right choice."

Two weeks later, Bill and I still hadn't discussed the session. I finally approached him. "I need to know what you've decided."

Bill shrugged. "I haven't made up my mind."

I took a deep breath. "Well, then, perhaps I'll do it for you. I've made a decision, and you need to leave — permanently."

Bill stared at me in shock for a moment and then smiled. "Let's go to dinner tomorrow and tell the kids."

I was sick inside, knowing I had taken the burden from him, and he was ecstatic. I knew it was time to move on and that felt good, but it was still so hard. I remember the kids crying for him every night, and it just tore my heart out.

At first, Bill was charming and agreeable to anything I wanted — the boat, the house, anything. Soon that charm turned to rage. He wasn't happy with the child support agreement the court invoked, he was less than thrilled about the fact that I was still living in his grandfather's house rent-free. He hated it when I was able to lease a car.

"What makes you think you can have everything your way?" Bill screamed in my ear while slamming me against the car.

"Let go of me," I hissed. "I've done everything you asked. I even took less child support than the court ordered because you whined about it."

98

THE TRUTH

His flushed face contorted with fury. "You are a b****!" He spit in my face and walked away.

The next day, someone at work pointed out my car was dented. I had no idea he had pushed me so hard. I called the police and filed a report. Bill was never physically violent to me again but would continue to spit in my face on occasion.

While we were going through our separation and divorce, many times I found myself desperate for money. The utilities were shut off when I couldn't pay for them. Bill paid his scant child support, but I never went back to court for a cost of living increase. If I would suggest returning to court to adjust the settlement, Bill would always reply, "Well, good. I'd like to increase my custody benefits, anyway."

It was interesting that even though he never paid what the court had actually ordered, Bill would retaliate with threats.

About six months after our final separation, Bill's family sold the house I was living in with the children. Bill took the kids with him for a summer visit, and I slept on the floor in a friend's vacated apartment. I had nothing but a pillow and blanket, but God kept me safe.

After a week, I heard back from the owner of a house in the country I had been looking at. It was a fixer upper house, but I was able to move in right away and finally have a place to call my own. It was really such a blessing as the children could attend a small country school that was small, similar to the private Christian school they were accustomed to.

Of course, we continued to struggle financially, and I even applied for welfare one time. I will never forget my experience there. The office smelled of the destitute people sitting on the benches. Most of them looked like they'd slept in their clothes or been in them for weeks. I choked on the lump in my throat and tried to find an empty chair. When they called my name, I cringed inside, knowing my shame was a matter of public record. When they asked why I was applying, I wanted to scream, "Because I'm going to have no food and my children need to eat!"

Why did they think I would degrade myself in such a way, if it weren't for my babies?

God always came through at the last minute with a job or some money, so I was able to avoid actually going on welfare. I was only a few hours away from the state's help, but I kept applying for work. It was my last interview of the day.

"So have you had any experience in real estate?"

I sat up and tried to sound confident. "My former husband was in real estate, so I know a little about what goes on. But I'm a great organizer, and I love to sell — anything."

"Well, you sold yourself."

Dan was a kind man, but his organizational skills were a nightmare. I soon discovered it was almost impossible to help him. I had been working for Dan for a short time when I left the office to go home for lunch.

THE TRUTH

I panicked and starting screaming because my car was missing.

"I know I parked it right here," I cried.

Dan came running out of his office. "Jump in my car, Lauren," he commanded. We drove down the street and there was the car. The man from the towing company had stopped to fill out his paperwork.

I watched in amazement as Dan flew out of his car and flung open the man's car door. "I'd like to talk to you about this."

The two of them argued, and Dan paid everything that was due on the car. I had to pay him back out of my earnings, but I kept my car. I knew it was God that had intervened as he had so many times before.

Dan was about 45 years old, and I soon discovered he hired me because he liked me as more than just an employee. When it became obvious he had a crush on me, I had to find another job.

Dan was nice enough to refer me to another real estate developer that needed someone to show their model homes. Again, I was hired because of my presentation and fired because they couldn't afford to pay me for the little work I was doing.

My family arrived for a visit the day after I was fired, and I was devastated. I knew God would find a way to help me, so I didn't let on to my family, and we had a wonderful weekend celebrating my mother's 50th birthday.

The following Monday, I began to hunt for a job again. Four different people told me I should try Davis Staffing. I finally listened, and when I went to Davis Staffing, I discovered a whole new world that I was meant to be a part of.

The owner of Davis Staffing was in when I arrived, and she seemed impressed by my professionalism. After meeting with her several times, I was hired as the office manager, earning $1,200 a month — not much more than I made when I was 17 in Alaska as a bank teller. I still didn't have much money, but I had a job, and for that, I was thankful. After the lease on my car expired, a friend loaned me a car to drive until I could afford to buy one. I drove around in an old 1980 Cutlass. It was a pretty humbling experience, and it was hard for me, but I knew things were getting better, and it was all part of God's plan.

The following Christmas, after I began my job at Davis, I put bikes on layaway at Wal-Mart for my kids. It was Christmas Eve, and I was heartbroken as I had no money to redeem the bikes. That morning, my boss gave me an envelope with $1,000 in it for my Christmas bonus. My hands were shaking as I lifted out the money. I could almost hear God saying, "Trust in me, Lauren, and you'll get through this." I rushed to the store to pick up the bikes, and when Christmas morning dawned, the kids were so surprised and thankful for the gifts. I'll never forget that Christmas!

I had thoughts of returning to Alaska and even went back for a few days to check it out. God seemed to be telling me the time wasn't right. Instead, I stayed in California. I increased the Davis Staffing business so much that the owner doubled my salary. By the following year, I was earning an annual salary of $30,000. When I more than doubled her business, my boss awarded me 25 percent of the profits. After seven years, I was earning $85,000 to $90,000 a year.

After the divorce was finalized, Bill still had his moments of insecurity and anger. His parents confided in me that, as a child, Bill was subject to fits of temper. I never saw that side of him until we started experiencing problems in our marriage. One time, when my daughter was involved in 4-H, we found ourselves in a horrendous argument over a sheep.

When a child participates in 4-H, they are required to care for an animal for months at a time. You keep the animal in good health and then show them for auction at the fair. This particular sheep was very nervous, and when sheep get nervous, their intestines tend to literally fall out their behind. It almost appears they are pooping, yet it is only intestines.

Bill helped my oldest daughter care for the sheep for months, and he prided himself on that fact. One particular weekend, the intestine problem had been exacerbated by stress. I was helping out with the sheep that day when Bill arrived at the stall.

"What the heck do you think you're doing, Lauren? The 4-H is my business," he snarled.

"Krissy needed help, and you weren't around," I snapped back at him.

He turned to my daughter. "You know better than to

SUFFICIENT TO **STAND**

involve your mother in 4-H business. You should have called me if the sheep was sick!" His voice was escalating and he was shaking his fist at her.

I stepped in between them. "You need to stop yelling and leave, Bill. Now!"

His eyes narrowed, and he spat in my face.

I quickly turned and grabbed my daughter's hand. "Run, Krissy, run."

Bill picked up a bucket and threw it at me. I ducked and the bucket hit my daughter in the back.

Krissy and I began to run in and out of the stalls, like a maze, with Bill chasing us.

"You get back here, Krissy. We need to talk about this," Bill hollered.

I was terrified he would attack me as he had before. Finally, I couldn't run anymore and turned to Krissy. "Go talk to him. It'll be fine."

Nauseated from fear, I crouched over by the side of a building and wept.

Bill didn't do anything to hurt Krissy and even apologized later for his behavior. I knew he had seen my actions with the sheep as interfering in his relationship with his daughter.

I realized then he was the one that had missed the real meaning of a father's love, and someday, all my children would realize the truth. I would not allow myself to hate as my mother did. My children would never see in me the anger that I saw in my own mother. Of that, I was determined. Only through trusting God could I learn to let it all go, and I did. My burdens were finally lifted after that, and I knew the right decision had been made.

I was a single parent whose life revolved around my children and my work. I would only date or make plans every other weekend when my children were gone. One Saturday night, after getting off work at 10 p.m., I stopped at the grocery store. After shopping, I decided to rent a video.

This is so sad, I thought to myself. *Saturday night and I'm grocery shopping and looking for a video to watch alone. Exciting.*

The manager had just gotten off work and was also perusing the video section. Many times, he had greeted me when I would stop in to shop, and we'd engaged in some pleasant conversations over the previous two years. "What are you up to, Lauren?"

I thought it a strange question. After all, we were at the video rack. I smiled back at him. "I'm just picking up a movie to watch."

He smiled back and nodded his head toward me. "All alone?"

"Looks like you might be doing the same," I quipped.

"Matter of fact, I am. Perhaps we should watch one together."

I was a little surprised and actually dumbstruck. The old smile routine was all I could do and pretend the comment never happened. He and I had conversations off and on in the store, but I had no idea he was even single.

He told me later, after we started dating, that he made

SUFFICIENT TO **STAND**

a comment to the checkout clerk after I'd left, "I'm going to marry that girl someday."

And he did.

Trevor and I were married in 1998 and moved to Fairbanks, Alaska, in 2001. I finally felt God was telling me it was time to return. Trevor is no longer in supermarket management, but he is fulfilling his dream of being a tennis instructor. We have two boys, ages 4 and 1. Being a mom this time around is so unique. I no longer fuss and fret about stages that children develop. My older children adore their two younger brothers.

I was able to take the learning experience and knowledge from Davis Staffing and open my own staffing business with my two sisters in Alaska. We are still the same close-knit family we have been all our lives.

There are times when I still think about my mother and how much resentment I stored up toward her. The pain has now been covered over as a scab seals a wound. My prayer for myself and my mother is that the wound would heal from the inside and make it unnecessary for the scab to remain.

I'm not sure if my mom has ever come to the place of examining herself and the bitterness and inability to forgive that has overshadowed her for so many years. Her first marriage to Roy ended in divorce in four years. She remarried within a day of her second divorce. That marriage, however, has remained intact for more than 24 years. My mother is a wonderful, beautiful woman, yet the anger she nurtures has taken away her ability to truly give

THE TRUTH

of herself.

The first few years Trevor and I were married, I endured some difficult self-evaluation. There were times when I could have fallen back into the same old trap of needing Trevor to be what I thought he should be. But I already decided never to go back, never to look at him to change, but to look at myself first.

If I had entered into my first marriage with that attitude, perhaps I would still be married to Bill. When we point one finger at someone else, we point three toward ourselves.

Looking back at my relationships and my relationship with God, I can truly say if you do the right thing, the right thing will happen to you, because God will do the right thing by you. I believe we all need to examine our own hearts and ask what we can do better. Those changes are very hard to make, but once you do, you learn to start giving when you thought you should be receiving. God is so amazing because no matter how many times we come to him, it's always the same. What you can do for others provides you a healing experience, and you are set free.

The Bible says, "You shall know the truth and the truth shall set you free." I found the truth when I let go and let God take my heart. I still struggle like everyone else, but that truth has made me whole; that truth has changed my life and set me free.

TO NEVER THIRST AGAIN
THE STORY OF AUBREY
WRITTEN BY JAMES R. WALSH

The San Antonio summer was hot and dry; Alaska couldn't have been farther away. I was with my dad and soon, I thought, I would be with him for good. By "for good," I mean away from my mother. Away from Alaska. I had been looking forward to getting away that summer all year long. For the first half of the summer, it was everything I'd hoped it would be.

I think everyone has "that summer." You know, the summer when girls get breasts. Boys get a wet dream. The kind of summer where you wear a halter top, smoke a pack of cigarettes, talk to boys till 2 in the morning. The kind of summer where you lay by pools, play never-ending hours of video games (so much so that when you close your eyes, you can still see the 16-bit pixels flashing); the summer when eyes notice you; the summer when your parents don't understand anymore, adulthood feels closer and farther away than it ever has or ever will feel. The kind of summer when you decide you don't want to be fat, and you survive only on Saltine crackers, Doritos and Dr. Pepper. You know, *that* summer.

We were all military kids, my summer friends and I. They lived across from our building, and we spent the whole summer together. I was the cool girl from Alaska.

"Do you ride dogsleds?"

"No," I'd answer.

SUFFICIENT TO **STAND**

"Do you live in an Igloo?"

"No."

"How is it living in the dark all the time in the winter?"

"Well, there is light for about six hours. And yes, it is depressing, but you get used to it."

You don't get used to my grandma, though — when she moved into our house, her presence changed everything. She was extremely overweight ("You'll look like her someday," my friends and family would say). Ever since she moved in with my mom and me, there was an uneasy tension. A disastrous laser eye correction surgery left her mostly blind. After that, her disposition quickly turned dark and depressing. I tried to avoid her as much as I could. My mom and stepdad seemed to fight all the time.

Visiting my dad that summer was a chance to get away from it all. It felt good to be on my own. My dad let me wear garments my mom would never let me wear. My only chores were to prepare dinner and wash the dishes, which left me lots of time to hang out with friends. I was in eighth grade and most of them were sophomores in high school.

"Hi, is Earl home?" Earl was one of my good friends who lived across the way. We hung out all summer. His family had a big-screen TV — one of the late-90s boxy ones that looked like a fridge. We didn't even have cable at my house.

I bought a cranberry-plaid shirt at the mall, the kind that would have sent my mom grabbing for her rosary. It was open in the back and bore spaghetti straps (not even thick spaghetti straps; we're talking rice vermicelli straps). With that shirt and my short shorts, I was sure I was every 14-year-old Texan boy's dream.

"Oh, hey," Earl's brother, Sam, answered the door. Sam worked at Burger King and was a senior at our high school. He hung out with us sometimes, but I didn't pay much attention to him.

"Is Earl in?" I asked as I noticed his eyes looking me up and down.

"Yeah, come on in. I'll go get him."

I walked in and plopped down on their blue suede couch in front of the big screen.

I waited patiently for a few moments; I didn't really hear any talking upstairs. He was gone for three minutes before he returned. "Where's Earl?" I asked.

"It doesn't matter," he dismissed. "I've been looking at you all summer."

"Oh."

Was that a compliment? What do I say to that?

"Have you ever had sex before?" he asked, sitting down on the couch next to me.

"No, I don't know that much about sex, really." My face was flush, and I started feeling really uncomfortable.

"So, you're a virgin?"

"Yeah, I haven't had sex," I told him.

"Do you feel like fooling around?"

"No." I couldn't believe he asked me that. "Listen, is your brother home?"

"No, nobody is home." He moved closer on the couch

and put his hand on my bare leg.

"I'm going home. My dad is really upset with me, and I could get in trouble."

"It won't hurt," he coaxed. "It'll just take a little bit, don't worry."

"I need to go home now," I asserted.

He pushed me by the shoulders. "It'll only take a moment, don't worry."

He pulled my pants down, and I closed my eyes. I was crying. It hurt like nothing else — the worst pain of my life.

I never should have come here; I never should have come here. Why is this happening? Do I scream? What do I do?

When he finished, he stood and walked to the bathroom upstairs.

Is it done, can I leave? I thought. I didn't know what to do.

Listening to him in the bathroom, I decided I would run out the front door.

It took me less than a minute to arrive home. My stepmother's car wasn't in the driveway, and my stepbrother was out riding his bike.

Who do I tell about this? Earl's dad is a military policeman; my dad performs gate duty — everyone would know. What would happen if everyone knew? Should I tell anyone or not?

I took a shower and used half a bottle of shampoo to clean myself, to wipe the memory away. I scrubbed my

TO NEVER THIRST AGAIN

whole body from head to toe and even tried to shave him off me.

Out of the shower, I walked to the park down the street and swung on the swing.

I'm not a virgin anymore, I thought. *It's gone. It's completely gone; I can't get it back.*

My mom always talked about just waiting until that someone special came along.

I should've been married; I should've been in love. That's how it's supposed to be.

How do I get that back? Am I a virgin still, even though it was taken from me? Am I still clean? My mom didn't wear white when she remarried. Will I have to wear a different color at my wedding? How could someone tell if you weren't a virgin? How could they see?

I was kicking the pebbles back and forth in the 100-degree temperature, asking myself these questions for what must have been hours.

"Where have you been?" was the greeting I received from my stepmom when I walked in the door. I hadn't prepared any dinner like I was supposed to.

"Sorry!" I yelled back impatiently.

"Where were you?" she asked.

"Just at the park swinging, and I lost track of time," I explained, deliberately cooling my tone.

"So, there's no dinner? Ugh," she sighed. "Let's just go to a drive-thru."

Later, she noticed the shampoo missing from the bottle.

SUFFICIENT TO **STAND**

"You're only supposed to use a dime- or nickel-sized portion — your hair isn't even that long, Aubrey."

"I know … I couldn't get the bottle to work, so I took the top off, and it all poured out."

Good cover, I thought.

I never told anybody about the rape. I explained to the boys I couldn't hang out with them anymore because my dad had seen a TV show about gangs, and he didn't want me to hang out with anyone black. Another good cover; it worked. I felt bad about the younger brother I was friends with, but it was the only thing I could think of.

I returned to Alaska when the summer ended. A few months later, a judge decided my mother was better able to raise me than my father — I was devastated and completely depressed.

I started taking my sister's Ritalin. It felt like speed. My eating habits turned into a case of anorexia, although I didn't know the word at the time. I only ate at dinnertime when I was forced to and spent all my lunch money on shopping. My sisters and I started drinking all my mother's alcohol and blaming it on my grandma.

"Wow, there's a lot of liquor missing!" my mom would say.

"Yeah, you know Grandma," my sisters and I would happily retort.

"She must have had a really tough day," my mom affirmed.

Like shooting fish in a barrel, I thought.

I bought all the things I wanted with my extra lunch

money. Ritalin gave me all the energy in the world, and I loved that, so I began looking on the Internet and reading about all the other kinds of pills that might be able to provide a temporary escape from my existence.

I was really upset about the rape, but I hid it away in more drinking and taking other people's medications. Then I started taking them at school to see what would happen.

The Ritalin would give me an anxiety attack, only with good feelings — like a good panic. My hands shook, and my heart beat so loudly that, if I was quiet, I could hear it over the white noise in the classroom. When I swallowed the pills without eating, I could feel the blood rushing through my veins. Sooner or later, I was skipping more class than meals.

I knew something was wrong when I passed out at lunch one day. One moment, I was talking with my friends, the next, I fell on the floor. My friends slapped my cheeks; I came back from the blackout.

"Are you all right?" they asked. "Should we call the nurse?"

"All I need is some Dr. Pepper," I replied, a comment that might have been funny under different circumstances. I was okay after that; I just needed some sugar fuel.

My ideal weight and personal goal was 75 pounds. Seventy-five pounds was just an arbitrary number, I don't know where it came from. I widdled myself down to 82 pounds, 80 in the morning (standing at 4'8"). I wouldn't stare in the mirror. It was a scale numbers game. Our high school was the state champion for wrestling, so nobody really asked questions about weight.

If boys can go crazy with their weight for some ridiculous sport that doesn't even matter, why can't a girl starve herself to look beautiful and have friends?

I could still pinch the skin above my eyebrow — fat. If I couldn't drop to 75 pounds, at least I wanted to reach the point where I couldn't pinch my forehead skin. Of course, now I know that everyone can pinch his or her forehead skin.

In December of my freshman year, I was raped again.

In church, during Christmas Mass, was the first time he kissed me. I was 14 and he was 23. My stepdad and his mother worked at the church, so he was a good friend of the family.

"Daniel kissed me," I told my stepsisters. I expected some kind of shock, some kind of disgust.

"Whoa!" They were both impressed.

"This hot 23-year-old man kissed you? Nice work!"

I felt bad for him, actually. He had gotten a girl pregnant and felt obligated to marry her, even though he didn't love her.

I was volunteering at a hospital when he showed up one day to bring me lunch. I followed him down to his car.

"Do you want to park at the field across the street and enjoy a hamburger with me?" he asked.

Ugh, hamburger and fries ... I felt guilty eating them.

"The patients are going to reel away from my onion breath," I joked. He leaned over and kissed me. I was nervous and didn't know what to do. It brought back all those memories of the base in Texas. "I think I should get back now," I replied. "You have a wife and a kid …"

"It's okay," he tried to console. He unzipped my pants and slid his hand in.

I couldn't go anywhere; he locked the doors. He climbed on top of me on the passenger seat and unbuttoned his pants, and then I felt that pain again. I closed my eyes and cried. Again.

That awful feeling.

I left when he finished and sat shaking in the hospital lobby until my mom came to pick me up.

I kept it a secret, and I wanted to die. I was in a depressed daze. Sooner or later, taking a pill here and there wasn't good enough. I wanted to end my life, but I wanted to leave some chance for intervention if it was meant to be that I should live.

In the bathroom, I found some Vicodin. About 15 pills were left in the bottle (one of them could make me fall asleep, completely knock me out). I swallowed them all. I then ingested some Ibuprofen. A handful of little aspirin came after that. My mom was at wrestling practice, my dad was busy upstairs. My sisters were busy downstairs. I don't know how I ended up there, but eventually, I found myself at the bottom of the stairs. I knew I should have felt pain, but I was numb and complacent. It was as if the pain was happening in another body, 100 miles away.

My sister heard me fall and noticed the bottle of pills that fell down with me.

SUFFICIENT TO **STAND**

"Oh, no; oh, no!" she screamed, running upstairs to retrieve my stepdad. "Dad! Dad! You have to come downstairs, something's wrong with Aubrey!"

My stepdad ran downstairs, saw the bottle of pills and asked what I had taken. I was unresponsive. He was yelling at me frantically, "What kind of pills? Aubrey, what kind of pills?" He called my mom's cell phone, threw a jacket on me and out we went into the 40-degrees-below-zero weather. "Stay awake, just stay awake," he commanded as he put me in the truck passenger seat. My eyes were closing; I was drifting away. "You have to wake up, you have to wake up!" he repeated urgently.

"I don't have anything to say," I mumbled.

"You have to stay awake."

He was nudging my shoulder at a stoplight. "Leave me alone, stop, stop …" I trailed off, drifting in and out. I was very hazy and relaxed and tired. My mom was waiting there; she was obviously upset, I could tell even in my grogginess.

"What's wrong? What's wrong?" she pleaded. "Why didn't you talk to me or tell me what was going on?"

I sat down; they didn't know what I had ingested. We were waiting for a few minutes in the lobby of the emergency room when my stepdad finally yelled, "She's overdosed, and we need to get her pumped, now!"

The nurse rushed me through, announcing over the intercom that this was a code red. The doctors came rushing. My body was so numb, I didn't feel the IV being inserted in my veins.

TO NEVER THIRST AGAIN

"Swallow," I heard from some distant state of consciousness.

The pump went down into my mouth. All the charcoal rushed into my stomach; it tasted like metal and dirt and sand. My stomach filled up more than it had since I stopped eating.

"Swallow again," the doctor directed. Out came the tube with black molasses gunk and a spot of blood on it. After that, I was all right to return home. My parents put me in the guest bedroom.

I couldn't take that gunk in my stomach anymore. I went to the bathroom and threw up into the toilet. It sprayed out of my mouth into the pure white porcelain bowl. My mom held my hair back. I stuck my finger down my throat because I could still feel it in there.

"You need to keep that in there for a reason!" my mom yelled at me. "It's there because of the choice you made to do this." I threw it up anyway.

"You don't know what it's like!" Maybe I was talking about the charcoal, maybe the rape, maybe about what it was like to be me or maybe I was talking about everything.

That charcoal taste lingered in my mouth the next morning — for the rest of that week, actually.

My mom was sitting at the kitchen table. I grabbed orange juice from the fridge and sat beside her. "I'm depressed," I told her. I explained how I wanted to be with my dad. I wasn't feeling good about myself. I wanted to die.

"Pain was the reason I took the pills. Pain. It couldn't

be any simpler. I was sitting in my bedroom, crying. I thought that life isn't worth all this pain; it's not worth all this pain at all. So that's why I went upstairs and took all the pills. I took it all and that was what I wanted to end it with."

After the conversation, my mom interceded. So, then came professional help. Then came constant monitoring. I only had privacy for the bathroom; even then, my mom stood outside the door. The door always had to be open.

My mom put me in therapy. She didn't understand why I wanted to kill myself. She didn't know about the rape. My therapist told me to write everything down my parents didn't know about, and then she faxed everything (including what I wrote about both of the rapes) to my parents.

I am too good for this, I thought. *I'm okay, I'm not a loser, and I'm not a weirdo. I'm an okay person without this stuff.* I cheeked the antidepressants they gave me. I took them for five days and then simply quit.

"Well, it'll take 30 days for the medication to kick in," the doctor explained.

I totally faked the whole thing. The one day when I actually did take the medication, I experienced the one-in-a-million-chances side effect — jaw chattering. I approached the nurse, and she took me to the hospital, thinking I had overdosed again. Nobody believed me, maybe with good reason. The toxicity screen came back clear. They switched my pills (I didn't take the new ones, either).

A few weeks went by. I tried every drug during those

TO NEVER THIRST AGAIN

few weeks: meth, speed, ecstasy, weed — everything that didn't require shooting up with needles. It didn't take long before I hit rock bottom again.

I caught word of a party that would include speed and ecstasy — apparently, the girl had even brought the pills to school. They were in her backpack, and she sat next to me in first period math. During the time we broke up into groups to solve problems and review our homework, I snuck into her bag. I found the blank white envelope that contained all the pills. I snatched the envelope and placed it in my backpack.

In between classes, I swallowed all the pills. Every single one. I ate a donut with them so it would soak up some of the pills.

First came the shakes; it was worse than I had ever experienced. There was the high, sure. It felt great, but there was also a pounding headache. It got worse and worse.

"I need to use the bathroom," I told my science teacher as he was taking attendance before we went into the computer lab.

"What's wrong?" He knew about me, of course; my mom set up a conference with all the teachers after my first overdose.

"I'm just nervous about this big project we have coming up." My hands were shaking worse.

"Let me just use the bathroom, please; I just need a drink of water," I pleaded.

"All right," he consented. "Just meet up with us in the computer lab."

SUFFICIENT TO **STAND**

I ambled into the bathroom. The water felt good on my face. It didn't help much, though, because my heart was racing. I climbed down the stairs to the computer lab and tripped.

My head hit the concrete steps. It should have hurt more. Instead, it just added to the rolling snowball of a pounding headache in my brain. I decided I would skip class. I headed to my locker where there was a phone with which I could call my counselor.

I just wanted to talk to my counselor. I liked her. Or at least I could talk to the doctor who prescribed my medication. I could get one of them on the line. I could not, would not, call my mom. Never. She couldn't know I had done this again. At the phone, I collapsed, and my body began to convulse.

I was out.

The hall monitors were standing around me when I came to. They were blocking the area so other students couldn't see. I blacked out again, and the nurse approached me; she had a pen light and was flashing it into my eyes.

She was trying to talk to me really loud. My pupils were so dilated, the brown of my eyes could not be seen. The nurse tried to take my blood pressure. I could feel my heart from my arm, and I knew I was in trouble. All I wanted to do was talk to my counselor.

Why are you making a big deal about this? I thought, but didn't have the capability to say it.

When she tried to put the blood pressure cuff on me, I

TO NEVER THIRST AGAIN

ripped it off and threw it down the hall. "Don't call my mom," I cried. "Don't call her, no matter what you do. Don't do it!" My mom worked five minutes away.

"Talk to me. I promise you, I won't hate you, you're my baby. What did you do?" my mom asked me when she showed up. I didn't want to get the pill girl or myself in trouble, so I didn't give my mother or the school officials any information. "You have to help us out, you have to," my mom begged of me. Her voice faded away, and I was taken to the ambulance. My convulsions were so bad that they popped one of my veins from trying to set up the IV.

My body was numb, and I didn't regain consciousness until the doors of the ambulance opened.

"Do you want to drink the charcoal like a milkshake or receive the tube again?" the nurse asked me.

"You'll never forget this milkshake," she teased, pouring Hershey's syrup in the glass.

My mom and my therapist made the decision that I was going to attend rehab. They made the plane reservations from my prescribing doctor's office; I would fly to Bellevue, Washington, for a week-long rehab program.

Of course, I was completely against the decision, so much so that they slipped me a pill so I fell asleep. I was completely knocked out and woke up in Bellevue, Washington, in my room. Not only did I wake up in a completely foreign place, I woke up to a girl — my roommate — standing on a chair, hanging herself by her shoelaces. It was such a surreal and horrific sight.

I freaked out and thrust open the door to the hallway.

SUFFICIENT TO **STAND**

The Bellevue staff had anticipated me waking up; my mother and counselor were there, too.

My mom was allowed to visit me once a day. I was going to complete my school work there so I could be caught up when I came back.

I spent a good amount of my time there walking in nature. I spent time reflecting on who I was, who I wanted to be, all the things I had done. Instead of hiding from everyone, especially from myself, I started coping with both of the times I was raped. My parents even prosecuted the man from church who raped me.

I learned what anorexia was — it was such a relief to have a word for what had been troubling me, for what had afflicted me. My sickness and state of mind wasn't some intangible darkness, something that no one else felt. It wasn't something that could not be explained or dealt with. It had a name. It had pamphlets. It had been studied. They gave my parents information about it. They were going to discharge me, but I approached my mom with a confession I almost couldn't admit to.

She was visiting me one night when I looked at her and told her, "If I go home now, I won't be alive in six months. I'll just die, I'll kill myself. I still don't want to eat. I don't know if I can go on. I feel like I can do it under a different set of conditions."

I couldn't stay at Bellevue because you needed to be a resident of Washington to stay there longer. We saw a video about a residency in Boise, Idaho. "That's where I need to go," I informed her, and that's where I went.

TO NEVER THIRST AGAIN

The hospital was right next to the state jail. My roommate and I watched guard dogs train from our bedroom window. While one view of the property was disconcerting, the other side had a beautiful view of the mountains. Tulips grow wild in Boise, and I instantly fell in love with them. I started to feel closer with God, too. I read a Bible from the library, but it was difficult to understand, and the Catholic priest who visited me was no help. He just wasn't interested in talking with me about my questions.

Through everything, my dad actually became a Christian. He started attending Max Lucado's (a famous contemporary Christian author) church. Max even sent me one of his books with some words of prayer and encouragement.

I was there for six months, from Valentine's Day until mid-August.

Many of my classes didn't transfer to my school back in Alaska. When I returned, I had to work insanely hard just to graduate with my class. I did nothing *but* school.

I was eventually employed at a local hotel working at the reception desk. That was my mom's way of getting me to stay out of trouble that summer — it actually worked out. I really liked working in hospitality.

There were so many rumors about me when I returned that I only had two true friends left at school — that fact made it easy to isolate myself and focus on my studies. I graduated magna cum laude.

I decided I would study hospitality and restaurant management at the University of Alaska, Anchorage. I

SUFFICIENT TO **STAND**

paid for my first semester and joined a sorority.

I also started drinking again, and my grades tanked. My parents considered it a "life-learning semester." Next semester progressed the same way, though.

Then, I met a boy. His name was Matthew; he was a sophomore in college. He was in a fraternity, had dark hair, was handsome — he was everything I thought I wanted. I was the "it" girl. I didn't go to class much. I thought I was in love with this guy. We were having sex every day, unprotected. Because of my eating disorder, I stopped having my period, and the doctors told me I couldn't conceive.

Memorial Day weekend, before my sophomore year, I found out that my grandma died and that I was pregnant. I was 19 and pregnant; I couldn't believe it. My uncle joked with me before I left for college that I'd come back barefoot and pregnant. "Well, I'm not barefoot," I told him. It felt so awful to not succeed in school after I had tried so hard to graduate; it was disheartening to fall into my same addictions.

I visited Planned Parenthood and scheduled an abortion. I paid for the ultrasound. The father was going to pay for everything else. It was all taken care of. No one would even need to know. I flew home to Fairbanks.

The night before my scheduled abortion, I couldn't sleep. At 4 in the morning, I went into my mom's room. "Mom," I whispered. "There's something I need to tell you."

"Sure," she replied, sitting up in bed.

TO NEVER THIRST AGAIN

"Promise not to hate me. Or that you won't stop talking to me."

"Honey," she began softly, "there's nothing you can say or tell me that would keep me from talking to you."

"I'm pregnant."

"Are you kidding?" she asked seriously, praying, I'm sure, for a joke.

"I'm not kidding," I told her. "I have the ultrasound; do you want to see it?" I pulled it out and showed the picture to her.

"Do you know who the father is?" she asked.

"Yes, it's Matthew!" I was surprised she would even ask that. "Don't you know me better than that?"

"I clearly don't know you as well as I thought," she replied.

"I was considering an abortion," I told her. "I can't go through with it, though. I want to keep the baby."

I looked up at Mom, trying to sound confident about my decision but desperately seeking her approval.

"I need a cigarette and a soda," she replied. Mom ended up driving to work at 6 a.m. the next morning when she wasn't scheduled until 8.

I went to work that day, too. When I returned home, she gave me a small bouquet of pink baby roses.

"We're going to do this," she told me.

"Do what?" I asked.

"Have a baby," she smiled. "We're going to have a baby."

I could feel all the weight just tumble off my shoulders.

SUFFICIENT TO **STAND**

I didn't go to college, of course. The father wasn't interested in me keeping the child, so we drifted apart. I endured a traumatic pregnancy and almost died; I had an emergency C-section because I fell into a seizure during labor.

After I gave birth, I continued working at the hotel. I was given a raise and a different position. One of my good friends at work, who was also a single mother, mentioned the church that she attended.

"I'd really like to hang out with you outside of work sometime. You should come to Friends Church with me," she invited. "The church has an aerobics class and a really great children's church."

All right, I thought, *I'll give it a try. What do I really have to lose?*

When I walked in the front glass doors of the church, I was so surprised. Everything was so different from the Catholic Church I had grown up in. The music was great, the people were friendly — you could even drink coffee in church! I found out there was a whole community of people at my work who were attending the same church.

It felt like I was home. I even ran into an old friend from high school; we began talking and recently started dating. I finally found a place; I finally found myself.

I started learning about the Bible and the passages started speaking to me. Passages like Romans 6:8: "But God demonstrates his own love toward us, in that while we were yet sinners, Christ died for us."

Regardless of what people think of abortion, everyone

TO NEVER THIRST AGAIN

can agree that having a child is a choice to live for another. Living for my child was the precursor to me living for God. When you are pregnant, you have to take care of yourself, you can't go out and get drunk — you have to plan for the future, you have to learn to be *selfless*. Your body is a temple for your child; your life is devoted to your child.

Becoming a Christian, my body became God's temple. Imagine the outrage a person would feel if he witnessed a pregnant woman drinking and using drugs. How much more, then, should a person be concerned if it is God who lives in her as she abuses herself?

Rehab helped me cope with my rape; it helped me stare my addiction to drugs and alcohol in the face and realize I was strong enough to overcome being destructive. However, it didn't change the fact that I was living for myself — I just wanted to attend school, have fun, fall in love and lead a normal life. As I learned early on in life, just when you want to live "normally," the world (and the people in it) can cause you so much terror and disappointment. I needed healing beyond what this world could offer me. Rehab quenched my thirst for meaning and belonging for a time, but it was only a matter of time before I fell again.

Jesus once told a woman at a well, "Everyone who drinks of this water will thirst again; but whoever drinks of the water that I will give him shall never thirst; but the water that I will give him will become in him a well of water springing up to eternal life."

We know from the story in John 4 that the woman had

SUFFICIENT TO **STAND**

many husbands (five to be exact) and was living with a man who was currently not her husband. I wonder if she walked to the well to get away from it all. I wonder if drawing water was therapeutic for her, a chance to get away from her life, just as my time in rehab was. However, with God, I found a rehabilitator who is perfect. One who knows me better than anyone ever will, who knows who I can be and who will help me achieve it.

I'm not saying people shouldn't go to therapy or rehab (just as Jesus is not saying people shouldn't drink water again). I get disappointed and even depressed sometimes, but I know my life events work out for my own good.

"And we know that God causes all things to work together for good to those who love God." (Romans 8:28)

Holding my new life, my son's life, in my arms, I see how wonderful, delicate and worth living life is. I see how God's purpose has unfolded for me. I pray now, as my pastor taught me, not just when I'm in crisis. I pray when I'm thankful, when I need patience, when I am glad to be alive. The more thanks I express to God, the more the wonder and beauty of life I see.

I started attending school again recently. I know God has wonderful things planned for me; I have lived apart from him long enough to know a lifetime of suffering and sorrow. I've experienced so much heartache in such a short time, but already, Jesus' healing and love have covered my mistakes and those made against me. I'm so excited about my future with God and have just begun to realize all the blessings I have in him!

THE BLANK CONTRACT
THE STORY OF ALEXANDER
WRITTEN BY JAMES RAYMOND WALSH

Perhaps there was a time when teenage boys found out about (or perhaps one could better say "discovered") sexuality through cave paintings, erotic tapestries, mosaics in bathhouses, statues of Venus, raunchy medieval plays, reading between the lines of troubadour songs, throwing coins in nickelodeons or sneaking into burlesque shows.

"Hey, I want you to come over and watch this movie," my friend Matthew asked me when I was 13. I went to his house, he put in the video and the world of sex opened up before me, more vividly and realistically than any other era of artistic depictions or fancy prose. Little did I know the addiction and dependency that first movie would lead me to.

I had just moved back to Arizona from Hawaii. The geographic change went hand in hand with the physical and chemical change of marching through puberty. Add the fact that, being my attention-loving, do-anything-for-a-laugh self, I made some enemies at my new school. The misfit kids gravitated toward me and I toward them. Matthew and Nate were my best buds. We guided each other in all the wrong directions. Matthew introduced me to porn. Nate was a couple years older, liked cool music and drank his parents' alcohol all the time. We watched porn movies every time we hung out, and well, it was nothing short of amazing to my 13-year-old self.

SUFFICIENT TO **STAND**

When Matthew gave me a knife and a porno, I was so excited that I wanted to share them, especially the video, with my older brother.

"Hey, come in my room," I beckoned him, "and check this out."

I pulled both items out of the drawer and showed them to him. Of course, he completely freaked out.

"I'm going to tell Mom and Dad," he threatened.

"All right! I'm sorry, I'm sorry," I pleaded. "I'll throw them away, just don't tell."

I fished them out of the trash that night.

It didn't take long until the group porno-watching experience became a more private affair. We watched movies together sometimes, but we mostly started trading videos in place of our group sessions.

Anyone born five years before I was probably would have seen a naked woman in a *Playboy* magazine discarded on the street or in the back of his dad's closet. My generation was probably the first to discover, from adolescence, porn on the Internet.

I honestly could not believe how wonderful and how transcendent was the shape and form of a woman. The Internet was the perfect mode to fulfill and over saturate all my curiosities about the other sex. A movie was one thing, but the Internet was on my own time — every body type, skin complexion, ethnicity, eye color or clothing style I could want was just a click and a few keystrokes away. With the Internet, I could really pause between pixels to imagine how soft her skin was, how it would feel to

THE BLANK CONTRACT

run my fingers through her hair. Nintendo games like Zelda and Mario were fun and had their place, but jumping on turtles does nothing to quiet the raging hormones churning within a teenage boy.

"What are all these sites on the Internet history?" my parents asked us one day, confusion quickly turning into fury.

I was the youngest of four kids. Needless to say, I had a knack for blaming my transgressions on them. I denied all allegations. You would think with all the brainpower it took to be so slippery and elusive, I would have figured out after the first two months of weekly accusations how to delete the browser history.

Even though the media of porn has changed through the ages, the worst fear of all fears for 14-year-old boys has remained the same — getting caught by their parents.

My dad was a huge military guy. You'd think I'd have heard his combat boots marching up the hallway with the laundry (even when he didn't wear combat boots, his feet hit the floor like they did). You'd think I'd have the brains to lock the door if I were going to pop a porno in my VCR while everyone was home.

I was watching a movie, and my dad walked in.

"Uh …" was all I could get out. He threw my nicely folded jeans on my lap and shut the door without saying a word. Then, half an hour later, we sat down to family dinner … I didn't utter a word.

That's not to say I wasn't punished (cringing at that moment for the rest of my life is punishment enough). I

SUFFICIENT TO **STAND**

still watched porn all the time, anyway. I even asked my friends over. We'd watch porn together and drink alcohol in my room. Alcohol was my next love. I never smoked pot or anything, but I did love the bottle. One good friend of mine was big into drugs, and I stopped being friends with him because of it. Never could take drugs — maybe it had something to do with the Ritalin they put me on in elementary school. The pill tasted like dirt and made me feel like a zombie.

For being a big family, people weren't around as much as you might think. My brothers graduated, my sister was always involved with sports, my dad had temporary military duty, and my mother kept plenty of friends to try and make up for the absence of companionship when my father was gone. I had all the time in the world for porn, uninterrupted. It was pretty easy to steal money from both my parents to spend on porn and booze, but I got a job at Dairy Queen for spending money, anyway.

That's where I first met Cait. I was 16 and she was 15 (although she had the body of a 23 year old). I had no idea why she liked me. I didn't have good grades, wasn't that good looking. I did play in a band, though. At the time, I thought that made up for the lack of brains and brawn.

It was time to live out my fantasies. I was reluctant at first, but sooner or later, we experimented with each other and stopped just short of "going all the way." She had everything. Long legs, curvy figure and beautiful blue eyes — she was the first girl I ever kissed. I actually learned how to kiss with her. I figured out I could basically get her to do

THE BLANK CONTRACT

anything I wanted.

We didn't do much together besides mess around physically.

We messed around in the morning at her house; she was so loud it woke up her brother. We always messed around in the next room or in the kitchen, just a few steps away from getting caught, which made the whole ordeal dangerous and fun.

We attended a Presbyterian church together. During Sunday school, we borrowed her mom's van and drove it somewhere secluded to have some fun. Our relationship was mostly physical. That's mostly what I wanted from it. At that age, it's easy to not develop a deep connection with someone — being in the same high school and liking the same band is connection enough.

"Alexander, I was with another guy last night," she admitted over the phone one evening.

Well, at least she told me straight up. She got sick of me; I honestly deserved it. I wasn't very nice to her. Not only that, but I manipulated her parents into spending a considerable amount of money on us.

After Cait, the majority of my time was spent drinking with Nate and my other friends. There were the girls, too: Amanda, Jessica, Rosalyn, Jillian, etc. They were all two-week flings. I did what I wanted and then went on to the next girl. Playing in the band and just being my goofy self, it was easy to meet them. I figured out how to manipulate them into fooling around with me. Then, it was on to the next girl, just as easy as changing the video in the TV or changing from one Web site to another.

I didn't feel a whole lot of guilt, either. My parents quit going to church. I had been raised in the church and had fond memories of it. I went to church a few times a week when I was 14. I didn't really take to heart anything, though. I remember how my youth pastor told me that he hadn't even kissed his wife until they married — ridiculous!

How sappy could their relationship be? It's a wonder they could bear each other's naked bodies long enough to crank out a couple kids, I thought. *Cool folks, though.*

David and Jessica were role models to me; I kept going back to church because of them. At the time, it just seemed like their romance was an impossible way to live.

It wasn't just in the sexual category that I was making mischief. I had always been one to slam my head on my desk or stand up on my chair and sing for a laugh (thus the Ritalin). When I was returning from a trip to Alabama, I decided I'd try and smuggle some fireworks back to Arizona. The Federal Aviation Administration (FAA) found them. We missed our flight. I pulled out all the stops for the letters I wrote the next couple of months to avoid prosecution and a fine upward of $32,000.

In high school, I embraced the role of provocateur to the extreme when I brought a confederate flag to school, wearing it around my neck. I wanted to be proud of my Alabama roots, but an African-American student's mom was not pleased. The principal called my parents, and my dad was even less pleased.

THE BLANK CONTRACT

Such antics did not replace my true love: porn. I was nervous when I graduated high school and attended the New Mexico Military Institute — all the computers were linked to the same server and were probably monitored by administrators at all times. Sooner or later, I figured out I could get "almost-porn." I planned my daily schedule around a couple visits from my hardware harem.

For a couple of years, I had been honing my guitar chops. I'd been getting really fast, listening to really hard music. My roommate and I were total opposites. He was a football quarterback, brats-on-the-grill, good ol' boy, but our relationship actually worked out pretty good that first semester. I thought I'd offer him inclusion in my hobby.

"Hey, Jacob, if you ever want any porn, just let me know. I have, like, a truckload."

"Well," he replied, being careful not to sound too judg-mental, "I actually gave up that stuff a long time ago."

"What are you talking about?" I asked, completely dumbfounded that anyone would give up something so good.

"I've been with a lot of girls, but I actually read this book called *Every Man's Battle*, and I don't struggle with that anymore."

Struggle?

I was pretty lonely. There was no sense meeting any girls in school because I had all the porn I wanted. Why settle for a real woman? There's so much maintenance. All that hard work just to get your biology on. Plus, there's the rejection, the heartbreak, the vulnerability and the loneli-

SUFFICIENT TO **STAND**

ness that comes with searching for someone — someone real.

"All right," I gave in, "let me check out that book."

I read a few pages, and it was interesting. Nothing life changing, though. We even read scripture together, Jacob and I. Arguing about what we read really made me curious to learn more about God, but I did nothing to pursue those studies after I left college.

I dropped out of college, and my dad let me move back home. I held two full-time jobs: one at Target and the other at Lozano's Pizza. Nate and I were still friends. At a party of ours, I met a girl as drunk as I was. Audrey was her name. We exchanged phone numbers, established a pretty good attachment and became exclusive. She went to the University of Arizona in Tucson. We met up every weekend, and I quit my job at Target to spend more time with her.

I lost my virginity to her in a tent during a camping trip. It was a spur-of-the-moment thing — we hadn't planned on it. Unlike other times, when I just wanted to get my fix, this time, I actually wanted to make our relationship stronger. I thought losing my virginity to her would cement our bond; I wouldn't have to feel lonely anymore, and she wouldn't leave me. I thought I loved her.

I fought with my parents that weekend, and I decided I would live up in Tucson for a while. Audrey was 20 and I was 18.

I stayed at Nate's house for a bit (Nate was going to

school up there then). When Audrey came over to visit, she passed me right up and went into the kitchen to talk to Nate. I knew they were talking about me.

She walked into the living room.

"Hey," I said. Things didn't look good.

"Listen, Alexander, I think we need to break up. Things are moving too fast."

Heartbreak. This was four days after I lost my virginity to her. She left and Nate and I made a trip to Safeway to buy a bunch of booze. The rest of the night went as follows: I got drunk as a skunk, watched porn on my laptop all night long with all of my friends huddled around, and then I made out with my buddy's girlfriend while he was at Taco Bell picking up a midnight snack for everyone.

Next came Vera; she was a virgin, though. We just kissed and talked.

Then there was my sister's friend Anne. I didn't want to just lose my virginity in vein, so I had sex with her the night we met. At that point, I was planning on going to Basic Training. I was watching as much porn as I could, knowing that I wouldn't get the chance in a couple weeks.

After Basic Training, I attended tech school. I met my next girlfriend during one of those new people briefings. Her name was Alexis, and she was wonderful, the kind of girl you'd take home to your mom. That semester, school was interrupted by Hurricane Katrina. Keesler Air Force Base is right next to Biloxi, Mississippi, so there was a whole semester of cleanup to perform after the disaster.

After Katrina hit, Alexis decided to spend the semester

SUFFICIENT TO **STAND**

at home away from the base. In the meantime, I hooked up with another girl who used my phone one night at a dance club and took all kinds of pictures of herself. She left her number for me, too. Her name was Tara. She was married. Tara was the kind of girl you lust after. I'd sleep with Tara and have Alexis as my girl I talked to and shared a connection with.

I didn't think much of the fact that Tara was married. I just didn't care.

One time, we were having sex in her bed when we heard a knock at the door.

"Tara, it's Tim," I heard from behind the door.

"It's my husband," she whispered.

I threw my clothes on so fast they were all on backwards. I exited the other door where my friends were watching TV in the living room. I checked my person for all my things, but when I got to my neck — *D*** it!* I had forgotten my dog tags on her bedroom floor. He didn't see them, though.

When she came out of her room, I asked, "Did he say anything?"

"All he did was grab my arm and say, 'Why can't you just have girlfriends? Why do you have so many guy friends?'"

It was funny at the time, but then they sought a divorce. It was pretty much my fault, too. I felt so much guilt. It was not as easy to erase as the Internet history cache.

I called Alexis after a month of not talking to her. I

THE BLANK CONTRACT

confessed half of everything: I had been with another girl (didn't mention the married part).

I never heard from her again after I told her all that. I couldn't believe I hurt her so much. I was transferred to Sheppard Air Force Base in Northern Texas. It was one of the loneliest times of my life. I looked at porn on my laptop everyday. I tried to call Alexis literally every day for a year.

She never answered or returned my calls.

Every week, I'd walk to the store to buy two porn magazines that came with a free porn DVD. I had been introduced on the phone to a girl named Eileen, and we talked pretty often. I gradually fell into having phone sex with her. I also talked her into picking me up from Texas and taking me to Arizona. We had sex at every stop during the trip. Maybe she thought we would actually be something, but when I came home, it was clear I was just using her.

I moved to Alaska in April 2006. It was there I was invited to attend a Christian group called Base Camp run by Bob and Ruth Ann Holthouse. They held weekly events and a weekly meal on Thursday nights.

Women were still my primary concern. I picked up a girl that Thursday night at Base Camp with the line: "Hey, want to come back to my place and play some Super Nintendo?"

It was a short fling and only held off my deepening loneliness so long. She was a Christian girl, too. I felt so guilty for ruining her spiritual life right in front of the couple who ran Base Camp. It seemed that way to me, anyway. In my mind, I took full responsibility. God worked it out for her, though, because after we spent our last night together, she went out with the man who would become her future husband a year later.

Who would have thought?

My sex life came to a halt, and I turned back to porn. I developed a crush on a girl named Christy.

"Know why you aren't supposed to drink from this end?" I asked her, pointing to the bottom of my cup.

"Um, not really." She had a confused look on her face.

"Because of this." I attempted to drink my Coke from the bottom of the glass and, of course, it all spilled out of the top onto my uniform. She laughed. I knew I was in … or so I thought.

She was such a good Christian girl; I was paralyzed by how much she was in love with her Lord. I was always mad at her and once even cussed her out because I couldn't get what I wanted.

I had another brief shallow sex fling after that before I decided I'd just abandon women and take up porn and alcohol again. I quit going to Base Camp. I was drinking all the time; I lived for the weekend. I started amassing so many magazines, DVDs and videos, it was nothing short of a library. I was consumed by lust and self-fulfillment.

One day, while driving home after work, my mom called and told me my remaining grandfather, who had raised her, had passed away. Then, just a few days later, my father was taking out the trash and couldn't lift the

THE BLANK CONTRACT

bag. He knew something was wrong, and my mom drove him to Tucson where he was rushed into emergency surgery on his heart. I told my supervisor about my family and flew home that day.

Dad had 100 percent blockage in one artery and 98 percent in the other. When I traveled home, I recall one of my first truly sincere prayers of my adult life: *God, please watch after us. Please consider my family.*

My dad was such a strong, solid man — I used to think of him as Superman; he truly could beat up any other dad on the block. At the airport, he was so fragile. I had never seen him like that. I didn't drink while I was home. I asked him for forgiveness for all those years of being a hellion. I appreciated my family's love more than ever — I also started considering my own life to be fragile.

I began to struggle more with sexual desire. By struggle, I don't mean "give in," I mean actually start to attempt to fight. I felt like I needed change. I started coaching hockey for kids and that led me to think more about families and what kind of man I should be.

While I was watching the NHL playoffs, Christy came by to invite me to the next Base Camp. It was funny, because I initially brought Christy to Base Camp, and here she was returning the favor a year later.

"I really want to go and change my life around," I told her. "I'm just worried; everyone knows about my drinking. Everyone knows about how I tried to get with you and how I corrupted that other girl. I just think everyone will hate me."

SUFFICIENT TO **STAND**

"That's not true," she countered. "Christianity is about forgiveness, and they will forgive you and accept you." She was so great with the Lord. She talked me into going and calmed my fears.

"Alexander!" Bob and Ruth Ann greeted me. "It's so good to see you. How have you been?"

Everyone was so welcoming there. I found out later Christy and Ruth Ann were praying for me that night.

"Come back on Thursday, all right?" Ruth Ann warmly invited.

Christy and I were driving Bob's four-wheelers at the next Base Camp Thursday night meal, when we were stuck in the mud for more than 30 minutes. She helped me get free; I thought it was a perfect metaphor for her bringing me out of my own personal muck and taking me to Base Camp again.

While a friend was driving me home from the bonfire, a song came on the radio. It was Shawn MacDonald's "Gravity." Leaning over with my head on the cold window pane, I prayed: *Jesus, teach me your words. Make them come alive in me. Have me live as you live. Wash me from all my sins and teach me.*

I was overwhelmed with feeling. Actual feeling. Not just the simulated feeling I had been arousing out of myself for years.

Through Base Camp, I signed up for a trip to visit Eagle, Alaska. It was an eight-hour drive through the beautiful mountains. Everyone in Bob's Suburban was talking about Jesus and the Bible.

THE BLANK CONTRACT

Come on, God, I thought. *I really want to change, but you have to make being a Christian more exciting than this. I have so many interests. I don't want to just sit around and talk.*

As soon as we arrived at Eagle, we started working. We rebuilt the pastor's house for the winter. We also rebuilt a shelter that had been a woman's home. She lived in poverty under a shanty roof of tarps since her husband had passed. Helping these people out, seeing their faith, I felt a spirit inside me that spoke to me and became my conscience, my lifeline. It was the Holy Spirit, the piece of God that lives inside of us. That's when I knew I had to commit my life. On May 26th, I asked the Lord to be my personal Savior.

How far will you go for me? That was the question that entered my head — the answer to my prayers was that question.

I started stripping my life of everything that was contrary to what God was showing me. I stopped cussing. I started weaning myself off porn. I put post-it notes all over my room with different Bible verses. I put them in my bathroom, in my kitchen and, of course, all around my computer. That's not to say I lived like a monk right away. I still experienced problems, but I started noticing a dramatic change in myself.

I wrote on my arm one day: *Does it honor the Lord?*

I used that standard to purge my life of all the things that were harming me, holding me back from becoming the person God intended me to be. Like it says in Ecclesiastes 11:9: "Follow the impulses of your heart and the desires of your eyes. Yet know that God will bring you to judgment for all these things."

I went for two months without even looking at porn. I did go crazy and eventually cave in, but that doesn't mean God doesn't honor that I was living for him, finally. I also respect and appreciate God's design in women — I don't see them as objects to satisfy my selfish desires and needs anymore.

The chaplain on base eventually asked me to be the manager of the North Star Café, a Christian coffee shop with pool tables, Xboxes and a kitchen area that served milkshakes and cookies.

I started denying myself things that were getting in the way of God. I decided I would fast from my cell phone because I was using it too much — I was relying upon it in the same way I had relied upon porn, to ward off loneliness.

I was going crazy for the month and a half I didn't have access to my phone. When I finally felt like the fast should be over, the first call I took was from the chaplain telling me that we were given more than $8,000 to spend on the café! It was everything I wanted and needed in my life at that moment.

I finally read *Every Man's Battle*, the book my roommate, Jacob, lent me in my first semester of college, and it was a great help to me. I also read a book called *Boy Meets Girl* and learned how God wants me to behave with any woman I'm interested in spending the rest of my life with.

THE BLANK CONTRACT

I decided that, like my youth pastor I ridiculed when I was young, I would not kiss my future wife until we were at the front of the church and pronounced husband and wife. I know that kind of rule might not stand for everyone, but after a life of so much impurity and lust, that's how I wanted my romantic love to develop.

When my brother, who had been serving in Iraq, returned home, we headed out on a 1,500-mile road trip around Alaska. I wasn't sure how to tell him about all the things that had been going on with me. My whole life had changed.

"There's something different about you; what's different about you?" he asked me. I hadn't said anything about it.

"What do you mean?"

"You're … more content. I've never seen you so content."

"I'm a Christian now," I explained.

My brother experienced horrible things in Iraq; I think some time together in the peaceful wilderness was what he needed. If I hadn't become a Christian, who knows what kind of brother he would have come back to. I would have been more negative and bitter about life than ever. Instead, I was stable. Maybe it rubbed off a little.

My brother traveled back to Arizona to the funeral of a good friend and fellow soldier who died from alcohol poisoning after they both drank too much one night. After the funeral, he kept attending church, and I hope God will continue to touch his heart and allow me to be an example to him of what God can do in your life.

I've started writing for God, too. Before, doing artistic things was just a way for me to channel my angst and loneliness. Now, art in the form of music and poetry is a great blessing, an enhancement to my life. I read through the dictionary and found words that applied to God, and this is what I created:

Him from A to Z

You are the Affinity of Archetypal Affection
You are the Ballast of Balance
You are the Dative Bond of Diversity
You are the Equilibrium of Existence
You are the Fathoming Father of Focused Freedom
You are the Graticule of our Gratitude
You are the Heartthrob of a Happy Husband
You are the Indemnification of the Insufficient
You are the Juxtaposition of Judgment
You are the Key to the Karyotype
You are the Lyrics of Lovers
You are the Man for the Matriarch
You are the Narrator
You are the Omnipotent Orchestrator
You are the Pestilence for our Pantomimed Purpose
You are the Quench of our Question for Quality
You are the Rector of Rhythm for a Relationship
You are the Seed for Science
You are the Thirst for Thoroughbred Trust

THE BLANK CONTRACT

You are in Us
You are our Valance of Virgin Values
You are the Warrant for Every Weakness
You are our Xanadu
He is the Yare for You
He is our Zeal and our Zephyr.
The Spiritual Zygote.
He is our Zori for our passageway to Zion.

Recently, when I was praying, I felt I should not eat until I was baptized. For a week, I didn't eat. I ended the fast on a Wednesday and was baptized that Sunday. For some reason, on Sunday morning, I checked my junk mail. There I found the e-mail Jennifer Wade from Good Catch Publishing sent to me on the Wednesday I had quit my fast — my story was selected to be a part of this book! When we are patient and listen to God, things work out much better than we could have ever imagined.

During my baptism, I joked with the pastor, "Hold me under the water a little longer for how many sins I've committed!"

Many religious leaders say that porn will lead young people to become carnal beasts for sex. Porn will turn men into insatiable sexual vampires, lurking the night for sultry pleasures. Nothing could be further from the truth. Porn, if anything, destroys your desire for a real woman.

Why deal with a real woman? Who wants a woman who has bad breath in the morning, who has parents you have to meet? Who wants a woman who may break your heart (which is much harder to clean than your history folder), a woman who has stubbly legs in the winter, a woman who has wants and needs and desires you have to fulfill? Women watch plenty of porn, too, so the same could be said of the inconveniences of a real man.

The point of my story is not for parents to always act suspicious of their teenagers or pry into all aspects of their private lives. A life devoid of freedom is more harmful to a developing adult than anything else, including porn. God warned Adam and Eve of the death that would result from eating from the tree — he didn't block off the tree under password protection.

The point of my story is that real relationships with real people begin with a real relationship with a real God. I needed to live my sexual life, considering God's plan, before I found sexual fulfillment in love with a woman.

Don't look to me as someone who is over an addiction, or some spontaneous monk who sins no more because he prayed some magic prayer. I sin. I sin on a daily basis. It isn't always the same sin, but I do sin. Philippians 6:1 reads: "For I am confident of this very thing, that he who began a good work in you will perfect it until the day of Jesus Christ." In other words, despite my shortcomings, I know God continues to work with me.

The best way to make a contract with God is to make a blank contract. When I decided I wanted to change, I put all my desires and hopes in without completely understanding where I was headed. I tried to find fulfillment in women, sex, garnering attention and drinking alcohol.

THE BLANK CONTRACT

There was no true, lasting fulfillment in any of those things. All of the physical satisfaction it gave me ended up making me more empty and lonely than I was before. I signed a blank contract with God, leaving everything I had, and from that, he blessed me with peace, true understanding and the hope (and life experience) "that all things work together for good to those who love him." (Romans 8:28)

BELIEVE IN ME
THE STORY OF AMY
WRITTEN BY MATT NORMAN

"Thank you, Ron." I smiled as I took the hot cocoa he offered. Ron always treated me as if I were an adult. At home, I was the baby, the youngest of three siblings. At Ron's, I was treated almost as an equal, even though I was only in third grade and he had finished high school and lived alone in his own small cabin.

Still feeling a chill from the long ride on Ron's airboat, I held the steaming cup to my lips as I walked around his cabin. I'd been there many times before, and as always, my interest was drawn to the bright, glossy pictures that smothered every wall. The pictures all showed beautiful women, women such as I had never seen in person. Each one was tall, thin, heavily made up — perfect. They were also all naked.

"They're so beautiful!" I exclaimed. "Do women like this really exist?"

"Sure they do, Amy," Ron answered. He took a seat on his bed and then looked at me with a smile.

"Why don't you take your clothes off, honey? I bet you're beautiful, too."

Ron often said this, and I always did as he asked. Once I was naked, I would pose like the women in the pictures, and he would just sit on his bed and gaze at me. The admiration I saw in his eyes made me feel I really was beautiful.

"You'll be just like those women someday, Amy."

SUFFICIENT TO **STAND**

I hope so! I thought. That, I decided, was my dearest wish.

From Ron's cabin, it was a short walk along the river to get back home. Instead, though, I started through the woods toward the home of our next nearest neighbor, Mr. Meyer. The forest was dense, but I knew every path.

Midway, I paused, unsure of whether I really wanted to go on. Mr. Meyer was a nice old man with a beautiful home, and every time I visited, he would give me money to buy candy. But to get the money, I would have to play the "raining money" game with him. He would take me to his room, turn off the lights and throw a handful of change in the air. I was allowed to keep whatever money I could find on the ground before he turned the light back on. It was a fun game, but sometimes, while I was crawling around searching for the coins, he would touch me in ways that felt strange. I wondered if I should ask my mother or father about this, see if they could explain why he touched me that way.

It was a beautiful Alaskan summer in the Land of the Midnight Sun. Mom was always saying if it weren't for the long, harsh winters, everyone on earth would move to Alaska.

Mom is always right, I thought to myself.

Now I was reaching the point where the woods gave way to my mother's flourishing vegetable garden. Here she grew just about everything our family needed. The tomatoes were starting to turn a bright red in the late summer warmth, and the green beans were sweet and crisp. Beyond the garden, I could see our pleasant little cabin and the greenhouse beside it.

What a great place to call home, I thought to myself.

Unlike the other children I knew, my older siblings and I were allowed to come and go as we pleased, giving us the freedom to do our own thing. *This is good*, I decided. I walked through the door with a smile on my face. My father was back for a few days from his work up on the north slope of the pipeline. I saw him relaxing on the couch with a joint he had rolled from the dried leaves of the monster-sized plant he was growing in the greenhouse. My mother was busy cooking our supper, fresh Copper River salmon and veggies she had picked from the garden. I could tell from their faces they were happy to see me return.

"Amy, were you visiting the neighbors all day?" my dad asked.

"Just visiting Ron," I answered.

"Well, honey, don't stay out so long. I don't want you getting into trouble," my mother added.

"Okay, Mom." *Besides*, I thought, *in such a beautiful place with so many nice neighbors, how can I possibly get into trouble?*

***

"Hey, Justin, put on my song; you know the one!" I yelled across the room. I finished off my Lucky Lager, savoring every last minute of summer and the total freedom it brought me. In just a few days, it would all be over. I would be starting the seventh grade.

For now, though, we had an entire well-stocked bar, complete with jukebox and pool table, to ourselves. My friends Justin and Dennis lived here. Literally. Their mother owned the bar, and its back rooms served as their house. It was an old bar built in the 1940s, with a slamming KISS pinball machine. When she was away on one of her many hunting trips or vacations, they had free run of the place. And as for me, I was always free to do whatever I pleased, whenever I pleased. I just told my parents I was going to hang out; I guess they just assumed parents would be there to supervise.

We had always been good kids, so they trusted us. "No news is good news" seemed to be their motto. Both of them worked, so they were gone a lot, and when they were home, they were tired. We would eat dinner and they would go and do their thing, and as soon as they did, my friends and I were at the bar, drinking and dancing. *Partying.*

The doors were locked, and the jukebox was running. We were playing bar, and I was the bartender. I was 11 years old, mixing tequila sunrises, and I drank everything. *Everything.* I was a recent graduate of sixth grade, and I was doing shots of Wild Turkey, 151, Southern Comfort and chasing the shots with every kind of beer or with the newest sensation, wine coolers.

I snuck a few cigarettes here and there, but I couldn't stomach them. Then I came across pot. I was 11 years old when I rolled my first joint. I remember I was in our camper trailer with the neighbor girl when I smoked it. Like the drinks, the pot was free — stolen from my father's stash.

My favorite band was the Beastie Boys, and I declared my right to party. That was my motto, that was my music and that was my life.

And yet, something about it didn't feel right.

I was sick to my stomach all the time from eating too much and too fast. I pretended to have migraines because my head was constantly pounding from all the second-hand smoke I was inhaling between my parents and my own weed smoking. Meanwhile, my friends in the orchestra, where I played the cello, had no idea what kinds of monstrosities I was up to. I suspected if they were to find out, they would be shocked.

I felt there must be something wrong with me. I had felt it ever since I started school. When all of the other third graders were saying they wanted to be teachers or lawyers or nurses, I was telling the teacher I wanted to be a Bond girl or Daisy Duke.

An object of desire. Someone who gets attention.

Now, at 11 years old, I finally found some people with similar inclinations. They were a bit older than me. In fact, I met them through my older brother, but they were people I could be myself with. *Or forget myself with.* I couldn't decide which the case was. In fact, I was beginning to think there were two sides of me — the good me and the bad me.

SUFFICIENT TO **STAND**

All the bad me really wanted was to have some fun, to forget about the constant fear of being different, of not being good enough, or, most terrifying of all, of being nobody. I longed to be with people who accepted me. On my 14th birthday, I received my first bowl burn from the friends that I felt truly loved and accepted me. It was a symbol on my arm of initiation into an elite and very cool club. After that, I knew I was in with the fun crowd, and as I took another shot of Jack Daniels and got up on the bar to dance along with my song, I thought to myself, *What could be the harm in that?*

***

"Mom, all I feel like doing is just going to bed, waking up and starting all over. I can't concentrate at my school. There are so many distractions. I just really need to drop out of society for a while."

"So what are you trying to say?"

"I'm saying I want to try homeschooling. Please?" I gave her the puppy dog eyes.

My mom was skeptical at first. Could I be trusted to get up every morning and study on my own while my parents were both at work? After all, the whole discussion came about because I'd been caught skipping school. My friend decided to call in to a local radio show when we were supposed to be in class. Dumb move, but then, she had been drunk at the time. It came as quite a shock to my dad to hear our voices on the radio show called "Desperate

BELIEVE IN ME

for Dollars," telling the DJ we needed the money to bribe our brothers to forge parent notes for us to skip school.

Because of the extreme circumstances, they reacted with unusual severity. Still, they were under the impression that it was an isolated incident. For me, though, it was the last straw. I knew that for several years, I had been spiraling out of control, getting more reckless and self-destructive every day, and if I kept it up, I might not live through high school, let alone graduate.

When I explained to my mother just how serious I was about homeschooling, she agreed that it was a good idea. And with that, my short but disastrous high school career ended. At least for a while.

Since I had started drinking and smoking pot, I grew more and more disconnected and aimless every year. By eighth grade, I was spending just about every minute outside of school with my friends. I commuted with my dad to a junior high school on Eielson Air Force Base where my dad worked. After school and almost every weekend, my friends and I would drink whatever alcohol we could get our hands on — usually by getting some young G.I. to buy it for us — and we would spend all day bumming around the base drinking and smoking pot until my dad got off work and we were ready to drive home.

The summer before my freshman year, I spent all day, every day, with my friend June and her mother at their house on the base. June's mother had the best pot in the world, and she smoked it with us day and night. We went to the movies or sometimes just smoked in their base-

SUFFICIENT TO **STAND**

ment. Every once in a while, I called my parents.

"Oh, yeah, everything's fine, we're just hanging out in the basement, watching MTV." I didn't mention the tin foil on the basement windows or June's mom passing me the pipe.

Then I discovered diet pills, which quickly became my newest addiction. I would pop handfuls at a time, often in combination with pot and alcohol. I was used to being sick from drinking and binge eating, so it was easy for me to take the next step — throwing up after meals. I became very skinny.

I cultivated a new hobby as well: shoplifting. My friends and I were hooked on the rush of seeing how much we could steal, and it turned out we could hide quite a bit. I had enough clothes and cosmetics to start my own store.

At some point, though, it all stopped being fun, and it was just something I knew I could get away with. I knew my lifestyle was destroying me. I felt sick all the time, and I was always jumping from one boyfriend to another. I initiated serious physical fights with my siblings at the slightest provocation, including use of the phone. I stole my friends' boyfriends. I was disrespectful to my parents, teachers, bus drivers and all adults in general. I didn't want anyone telling me what to do. I became a very good liar. And all of it felt wrong.

I'm such a terrible person, I would think to myself.

I was starting to conjure up suicidal thoughts.

By high school, I became sexually active. Sometimes, I

was too wasted to think of using protection. I didn't really care, and no one else seemed to, either. It felt good to be so wanted. On Halloween, after watching the movie *Pretty Woman*, I attended school in lingerie and told everyone I was dressed as a call girl. When I drank, it was like an animal would come out from somewhere inside me.

So, while my parents probably saw homeschooling as a whim on my part, I saw it as my last hope. I threw myself into my correspondence courses and the days of isolation in my home that came with them. Away from the pressures and dramas of society, I was able to greatly reduce my drinking and pot use. I suddenly found schoolwork far easier than before. Where I had once struggled to eke out D grades, I was now acing tests.

In my solitude, I even began to enjoy nature again. Cutting through the woods on a snow machine, I felt sharp thrills of wonder that made me feel almost like a child again.

Still, I experienced a vacant, rootless feeling. There was a hollowness inside me I had previously hidden from myself with pot and alcohol. I was moody, and most days, I preferred not to leave the house.

Finally, I found something that filled the emptiness a bit, or at the very least, smoothed out my moods: my mother's Prozac. Pretty soon, I had my own prescription. It seemed that Prozac was the new miracle fix-all for Seasonal Affective Disorder, which is weather-related depression, a big problem in Alaska. But I was just trading old dependencies for new ones. Or, as it would turn out, simply adding another to the list.

Nevertheless, I was feeling like a new person, and my parents convinced me that by missing high school, I was missing the best time of my life. After two years of homeschooling, I decided I was ready to go back to public school for the second half of my junior year.

***

"Amy, how come you're such a witch? What were you doing at Jeremy's house last night?"

"It's none of your business, Alyssa. But just so you know, we weren't doing anything."

"Yes, it is my business. Jeremy is a good friend of mine."

"Meaning you want him, right? Well, he's not your boyfriend, so I'm afraid you can't control who he spends time with. Sorry."

"I don't care who he spends time with as long as it's not with you, you slut!"

I couldn't control myself any longer. I had tried so hard, ever since returning to high school, just to fit in. I resumed my regimen of diet pills, spent all my Permanent Fund Dividend money on clothes, tanning and getting my hair done and acted the way I thought I was supposed to, all so people would accept me. And it had all gone wrong. I got into several fights with the girls in my class. It was just too much for me. I was crushed. And now this tall, beautiful, perfect cheerleader was standing in front of me, looking down on me and calling me a slut. I couldn't take it anymore. I exploded.

I got up and lunged at her, grabbing her shoulders with both hands and shaking her. "Who are you calling a slut, you spoiled priss? Everybody knows you're just jealous!"

She grabbed me by the hair and pulled so violently that my head flew back, and I howled in pain. I responded by pushing her so hard that she fell to the ground, but she dragged me down with her. After that, we were locked in battle, rolling on the gravel, each struggling to make the other give up, but neither of us would. The fight was getting more and more intense. She was scratching my face with the fingernails of one hand, while the other hand was pulling back hard on my hair. Suddenly, it was as if my survival instincts took over. Before I knew what I was doing, I could feel warm blood all over my mouth and see it glistening in the firelight all over the side of her head. She was screaming in pain and fear. I jumped back, stunned.

What did I do? Whose blood is that? Then I heard the screams.

"Holy crap, she bit off part of Alyssa's ear!"

I sat there in total shock. It couldn't be. But then I saw that a piece of her earlobe really was missing. I was moving to help her when her friends grabbed her and pulled her away. From the raging bonfire party at Nordale pits, they drove her to the nearest hospital in Fairbanks. I was still sitting on the ground, trying to come to grips with what I had done, when some of Alyssa's friends returned.

SUFFICIENT TO **STAND**

They were looking for the missing piece of Alyssa's ear.

This happened shortly after the infamous incident involving Mike Tyson. Needless to say, the remainder of my senior year was tortuous. In the end, I didn't even graduate.

The following summer, I turned 17. I knew I needed a break and some adventure, so I convinced my parents to let me spend the whole summer camping in Denali National Park. It was beautiful, and I was determined to enjoy every minute of it. Still, as the summer moved on, I sunk further into self-destruction, desperately trying to understand, or at the very least, forget what had happened to me over the last year.

Every night of that summer, I sat by a campfire, sometimes with other young campers, just as often alone, drinking, smoking pot and popping handfuls of Prozac and diet pills. When my boss at work got into the habit of looking down my shirt and touching my butt, I didn't protest. I felt like somehow I deserved it.

The next year, I was able to earn my diploma at an alternative school by cheating on my economics final. Later, I moved to Anchorage with my boyfriend and started attending travel school. My boyfriend didn't smoke or drink, so I tried not to. For a while, things were going well.

After graduating from travel school, I was able to move from my job in an outfitting store to a better job in a travel agency. Still, in both cases, much of my income came from stealing from my employer.

I'm just a bad person, I thought. *I can't help but do bad*

BELIEVE IN ME

things. Why fight it? Once I accepted the fact that I was a bad person, I decided to leave my boyfriend, the only positive influence in my life. He was just too good for me.

***

I put down my bong and headed to the refrigerator. *I am starving.* But when I opened it, I couldn't believe my eyes.

"Hey, Mike, we're completely out of food. There's not a thing in the fridge or the cupboards."

"Well, why don't you run into town and bring something back?"

"All right, give me some money."

"Don't you have any money left?"

"No. Do you?"

"Not a cent. I've been broke for a week now."

"Great, now what do we do?"

Things had been idyllic up to that point. Living in the beautiful cabin by the lake that belonged to Mike's parents, the two of us spent all of our time smoking pot and thrashing on jet skis like crazy, out-of-control teenagers. Ever since his parents had left for the summer, we'd been living this way. I wasn't in love with Mike; I even knew that he saw other girls on the side, although I didn't let him know that I knew this. I was there because he always offered good pot. What he didn't always have, though, was food.

Once again, Mike got fired from his job with the family

SUFFICIENT TO **STAND**

business, and I was only working part-time at hockey games, and that was only because I could get away with going to work stoned. I smoked a lot of pot with my boss. My last paycheck had already been spent. Now, we were alone in the woods with no food or money.

"Don't worry about it, babe. I'll take care of it."

I looked at him skeptically. Laying on the couch, hung over and coming down from mushrooms, he didn't look fit to take care of anything.

We're such losers, I thought to myself.

But if he could come up with something, I wouldn't have to go to my parents for money, or move back in with them. I told him to do whatever he had to.

A few hours later, we not only had plenty of food, but a television and a stereo. It didn't take a detective to figure out he had stolen it all from neighboring cabins. I never protested. It felt wrong to me, very wrong. But then again, so did just about every part of my life.

Within a few months, Mike left for college, and I'd completely lost touch with him. I left my job at the hockey games as the beer girl and landed a full-time lead agent position for an airline. I was back living at my parents' house, and it didn't take long before I hooked up with the party crowd. By now, I had developed the habit of drinking until I blacked out. I found a new boyfriend, and after I got really drunk, he would share me with his friends. I was always too drunk to care. The next day, when I remembered what I had done, however, I would break down in tears. Even so, that night, I would smoke pot again.

BELIEVE IN ME

***

I thought long and hard before I spoke. Carl had just said goodnight to my parents and was getting ready to get into the bed we shared. I looked at him and wondered for the thousandth time how to tell him, whether to tell him.

Do I really know this man? He's 33, I'm 21. He's 6'3" and I'm 5'5". I've known him less than a year. He's never revealed his true self to me. Can I trust him? Or should I just end this now? But then what?

Since meeting Carl, life had been a blur. I met him while modeling for a Harley Davidson shop. He was modeling, too, and after fashion shows, he would take me for long, exciting rides on his Harley. At the time, I was in the process of spinning out of control.

One afternoon, I left a Memorial Day barbeque very stoned and drunk and got into my car, determined to drive to my childhood stomping grounds 40 minutes away. I drove through the night like a maniac in my '62 Impala, from Fairbanks through North Pole and past Eielson AFB, passing every other car on the highway as if it were standing still. After a while, I started to notice the people I was passing were looking at me like I was insane. I laughed and stomped down on the accelerator.

I was almost to my destination when I realized there were cop cars behind me. Four of them. They had been following me for half an hour and I, oblivious to their presence, had turned it into a car chase. It would be a long time before I would get my license back.

SUFFICIENT TO **STAND**

Luckily, Carl was there with his Harley to give me rides wherever I needed to go, which mostly meant taking me to work and to bars on the weekends. For the next six months, we were inseparable. I was on the back of his Harley, traveling all over the area, going out and drinking every weekend. I was a free spirit, and with my long blond hair and tight leather clothes, I was always the center of attention. Every weekend, I would go to the bar and drink until I blacked out, and I could count on Carl to get me home safely. Pretty soon, he had moved into my parents' place with me.

Even though it was our love of biking and good times that brought us together, I had come to care for Carl, and I could see he truly cared for me.

But is that enough? Will that withstand pressure?

I realized the time had come to say what I had to say. I also realized what I feared the most was his reaction.

How will he take it? How should I say it?

I decided to just come out with it.

"Carl, I need to tell you something," I began, looking at his face intently. "I'm pregnant. You're going to be a father."

"Are you serious, honey? Is it true? That's incredible! That's the best news I've ever gotten!" Carl exclaimed, unable to contain his excitement. I laughed at his enthusiasm in relief.

This is right. This is how he should react. Everything is going to be fine!

"Amy, make me the happiest man on earth. Marry

BELIEVE IN ME

me."

I didn't hesitate for an instant. "Yes, I will. I love you!"

***

I woke from my sleep being shaken roughly and so hard that my head was banging against the headboard.

"Get up and do something useful today! Be productive!" Carl was bellowing at me as he shook me awake, also waking our 1-year-old baby boy who was nestled up next to me. I could see anger and disgust in his eyes. This was how every day had started for me for several months. I felt a sinking feeling. No day that started with such pain could turn out well. My waking hours loomed before me like a long, bleak ordeal.

Nothing, though, was more terrible than those first few moments each day — waking up to a harsh reminder of how worthless I was, what a disappointment I'd become to my husband.

What a way to begin the day. When did my life turn into this?

I sat up, wiping the tears from my eyes. Oblivious to my pain, Carl left for work. It was good to be away from his abusive language and constant reprimands. We couldn't be around each other long before he made me feel worthless. But with him gone, the new house was so empty. I was alone there with my feelings of failure.

My only company was my baby, my precious Drew. Seeing him flooded me with joy. But at the same time, his

SUFFICIENT TO **STAND**

beauty felt like a reprimand. I could never be a good enough mother for such a perfect baby. I was failing him. When this feeling hit me, I headed for the bathroom. I needed something to take away this pain, and though nothing ever worked for long, I kept searching.

It was soon after Drew's birth that the depression hit. It was accompanied by drastic mood swings and anxiety attacks. First, I started taking Prozac again. Then, I started smoking pot. Finally, I added sleeping pills to the mix. Nothing helped. I was alone all day and night; I could feel Carl's burning resentment toward me.

Taking the prescribed doses of medication, I started to hallucinate, to see the walls move. I went from one doctor to another, and each one added a new drug to my regimen. I was looking for the right cocktail. Now, I was taking antidepressants, antipsychotics, mood stabilizers, anti-anxiety pills and sleeping pills. To this, I added pot every now and then. At times, I couldn't sleep, eat or even move. When Drew was a little more than 2, on most weekends, I started hitting the bars again. At home, Carl would glare at me with contempt. In the bar, I was again the center of attention, and the drinking would dull the pain. I would drink until I blacked out.

Why? I asked myself, desperately. *How did things get so out of control?*

I took a look around me. My home was so beautiful, and so much love had been put into making it. My entire family, along with Carl, had spent months putting every spare moment into our new home, and the result was gorgeous. The finishing, the tile, it was all nicer than anything I ever thought I'd have. And then there was my precious Drew. I had felt whole for the first time during my pregnancy with him. I quit drinking and stopped taking any drugs or medication without any difficulty. It was easy to do for my baby. But now that he was out, now that I could see him as a living, breathing human, I was overwhelmed with inadequacy and fear.

What if I can't be a good mother? How can I possibly be a good mother when I'm so messed up?

Carl certainly didn't help. I learned during our honeymoon he was addicted to gambling on sports. From that point on, he paid more attention to his gambling than to me. And soon after Drew's birth, he became verbally, and then physically, abusive. His mother convinced him I was doing a terrible job caring for Drew. Drew suffered several fevers, and Carl blamed me. I was starting to believe what he told me.

"Look at you. You've gotten fat and ugly. You're a terrible mother. How could I let somebody from such a family of losers be the mother of my child? What kind of wife are you?" I took his words to heart and fell deeper into my despondency. When I discovered he had begun viewing Internet pornography, I knew it was true: I was no longer attractive to him.

I am a terrible wife — a terrible mother. I am worthless.

I started to fantasize about suicide. I held unloaded guns to my head and visualized myself sitting in the parked Impala while it was running. I knew I couldn't do it, I could never leave my son, but I felt he would be better off if I did.

It's what I deserve.

One day, my mother stopped by to see how I was doing. Before I knew what it was she had come over for, she slapped me across the face.

"What are you doing to yourself, Amy? Get rid of all of this medication. Get your life back together. You're going to lose your child; they'll take him away from you and lock you up in a mental hospital. You'll never see him again. Is that what you want?"

I realized she was right. The drugs weren't helping me; they were making me worse. I began my attempt to quit. But Carl was still Carl.

One night, after another of our knockdown, drag-out fights, I locked him out of the house. He was stuck in the frigid Alaska winter, so he kicked the door down. When he stepped in, I could see unalloyed rage in his eyes. I ran to the bedroom and called the police. That was the end of our marriage.

He brought papers for me to sign declaring that everything was his. The house that I loved so much and that my family had built, the beautiful furniture they had given to us, our construction business, all of our money, our retirement accounts, everything. He told me unless I signed, he would challenge my custody, and I would lose any right to see my 3-year-old son. So I signed. I went back to living with my parents, without any money. But I could still see

BELIEVE IN ME

my son; every other week, he was mine.

***

I drove through the dark morning on my way to work at the travel agency. I was happy to be returning after my long sickness. I thought back to the moments in the hospital when it looked like the scarlet fever was going to win, when I was sure that I was going to die. I could still remember the desperate thoughts racing through my mind. I had wasted my life, and now that I finally had something worth living for, I was being taken away. As I lay there, the only thing I could think to do was pray.

Please, God, if you're there, change me, make me a better person. I don't know how to pray or what to pray for. The only things I've ever asked you for all my life were to give me a beautiful body, to make people love me. But now all I know is I want you to change me. I don't really know how to pray to you. I don't even know who you are. But I think I need you.

My temperature was 105 degrees, and I was hallucinating and certain I was going to die. But then the fever broke.

Did God save me? I wondered.

All I knew was I had a second chance, so I made myself a promise.

I promise I'm going to try to change my life. I don't know how, but I will try.

As I returned to work, I was determined to keep that

promise. I was sitting in the left turn lane on the Steese Highway, thinking this, when out of nowhere appeared a huge, white Ford extended cab truck, trying to make a turn on two wheels. It was clear he wasn't going to make it — he was going to hit me. Time seemed to stop. I glanced at the clock.

8:21 a.m., this is when I'm going to die. Oh, God, I'm going to die right here, right now! Please, God, I'm sorry, I'm sorry that I'm such a mess, but I don't want to die. I have a child, and he's so beautiful, please don't let me die.

The noise of the crash was so loud, it sounded like the whole world was ending that moment in an explosion, and the next thing I knew, everything was silent, everything was black. I couldn't move.

Am I dead?

This went on for what seemed like ages. But then I heard something. Sirens. An ambulance was there, and someone was pulling me from the car.

I'm alive. I can even stand up.

I looked back at my car and gasped in horror. It was completely mangled from front to back, no longer even recognizable.

How could I have survived that?

And behind my car was the truck, flipped up on its roof, and in front of it was a man lying face down. I thought he was dead. I turned my head, feeling sick. But then he stood up. I couldn't believe what I was seeing. It was impossible. He was yelling at everyone. He was probably hurt pretty badly, but he didn't know it. He was drunk

BELIEVE IN ME

and high on meth. I still couldn't believe it.

My God, I'm alive!

My back and neck were pretty messed up. I was in the hospital and in a lot of pain, but I refused to take painkillers.

I'm alive because I promised God I was going to change my life, and he saved me. And I meant my promise; I'm going to get better.

For a long time afterward, I was in a great deal of pain. But I stayed clean. And soon, I got a new job, working at my son's daycare center. It was a Christian daycare center; God had put me in a place where I could learn more.

Things were getting so much better. I purchased another car. I didn't make much money, and I was living with my parents, but I could see my Drew more. I saw him just about every day now. On the weekends, I stayed home with my son and washed laundry and performed household chores. I was keeping my promise. I took my job very seriously and went all out, making myself very available, and within one year's time, I got an offer I couldn't believe: my preschool wanted me to become a lead teacher!

Now I was in charge of my own preschool room. I have always loved rainbows, so my students became God's Little Rainbows. And all day, every weekday, we would play and learn. It was the greatest thing that had happened to me after Drew. I was happy. And for the first time, I felt I deserved it; I was keeping my promise and felt I deserved it.

SUFFICIENT TO **STAND**

***

"Sylvia, I need to talk to you."

"Of course, Amy, have a seat. Is there anything wrong?"

I sat down before my supervisor at the preschool. I still couldn't quite believe what I was about to say, but somehow, I felt it was what I had to do.

"Sylvia, I'm not going to teach anymore. I'm giving you my 30 days' notice now."

"What? Amy, you're so happy here, and the children love you! Why would you do this? Is there something wrong? Is there anything we can help you with?"

"I'm just going to do something different with my life. I need a new direction. I'm going to be a hairdresser. I have to make more than $9 per hour to make a living wage."

Sylvia looked stunned. "A hairdresser?"

Before she could try to talk me out of it, I got up to leave. "I'm sorry, Sylvia, it's just something I have to do. For myself."

I turned and exited the door so that Sylvia wouldn't see the tears welling up in my eyes. I was leaving my precious Little Rainbows.

I don't deserve them anymore. I was back to being my old self. My real self.

Earlier that year, I had taken a vacation to Ft. Meyers, Florida. My closest friend was getting married, and I was there to celebrate with her. I stayed there almost three weeks, and as soon as I arrived and met up with my friends, I was back to my old ways. I hit the bars; I got drunk and had sex. It seemed to happen automatically, without me ever realizing what was going on. By the time I got back, everything had changed.

I went back to my class, but I was no longer the nice preschool teacher with her hair in braids. Whatever had happened, the change was clear to everyone. Now the single fathers of children in my class were asking me out on dates. And I started going out again on the weekends. I felt that I'd fallen, and there was no way I could ever redeem myself again. The person that I had been, that I still pretended to be when I was with my class, was a lie. The real me was bad, and I couldn't live such a lie anymore.

I've failed again. Failed everyone — my son, my students, everyone who cares for me. And God. I'm beyond forgiveness.

***

"You sure are popular here, Amy. Every guy here is in love with you."

"Oh, yeah? Great. How about another drink, Al?"

"You sure you want another? Remember how sick you got last Saturday?"

"I'm positive. I'm just getting started."

Reluctantly, Al yelled to the bartender to pour me another.

Always watching out for me.

SUFFICIENT TO **STAND**

I could tell Al had a thing for me. Ever since I'd started coming to the country bar he owned, he had been paying so much attention to me. Then again, so was everyone there, the guys in particular. I was my popular, desirable self once again. Al even asked me to model in the TV ads for his western clothing store.

The bartender slid my usual in front of me. "Thanks as always, Al," I replied. For me, drinks were always on the house. And I made the most of it, drinking myself sick every Friday and Saturday.

Drinking to forget.

My day-to-day life at the hair salon was a kind of torture. The entire culture revolved around superficiality, around having the right hairstyle and wearing the right clothes. Everyone there looked perfect on the outside, however much his or her life might be in disarray. I fit right in.

I went back to my life of blackout drinking, pot smoking and one-night stands with a vengeance. And now, at the local country bar, I was the "it" girl. It was my old life all over again, and it was just as miserable as the first time.

"You look kinda sad tonight, Amy."

"I'm just wondering what I'm doing here. I have a son that I love at home. I really shouldn't be like this. But when I'm not here, all I think about is how beautiful I will look on the weekend, how much attention I will get. Al, what is wrong with me?'

"Well, tell me something, Amy. Do you believe in God?"

BELIEVE IN ME

"Of course I do. But that doesn't make any difference; I'm just not a good person. I've let everyone down, even God."

"I don't know, I think he'd be willing to give you another shot. You know, I just became a Christian a few months ago. I've been going to a church in the city called Friends Church. It's really helping me. I feel better these days than I have in a long time. Why don't I pick you up tomorrow morning and take you there with me?"

"Church? No, I don't think so. I've been to church. It freaks me out. I feel out of place. Everyone is so proper and elegant. And I can't understand anything the pastor says."

"Well, there's more than one kind of church. Maybe this one would be more in your lane. It's pretty different from other churches I've been to."

I could see that Al was getting pretty excited, talking about this new church he'd found. He was starting to become animated. I just found it funny that I was sitting there, drunk and wearing skin-tight jeans, talking about church of all things. I also knew there was no way he was dragging me to church. Still, Al was a nice guy, so I decided to humor him.

"So, what's so different about it?" I asked with a skeptical smile.

"Well, the music, for one thing. It's Christian rock. It's music that moves you on the inside and the outside."

I just nodded, thinking, *Okay, whatever.*

"And then there's the pastor. He doesn't really yell at

179

you or scream; he just talks about life and then shows you how the Bible relates."

At this point, I just wanted to change the subject. "Okay, Al, I'll go with you someday, I promise."

"Great! I'll pick you up at 10:30 tomorrow morning."

"10:30?" I was sure he was joking. My typical Sunday consisted of rolling out of bed at noon and then stumbling into the bathroom and puking in the toilet. Meanwhile, Drew would be in the other room, eating cereal and watching cartoons.

Al was a very persuasive guy, though, so the next day at 10:30, I found myself driving with Al toward Friends Church. I was nervous.

"How do I look? Is this outfit nice enough? Or is it too tight?"

"Don't worry about it, Amy. You look great."

Al and I walked in and took a seat. I couldn't believe how many people were there. I hadn't seen that many people in one place in a long time. The music was pretty good, too. I looked around and recognized a few faces. Then the pastor started talking. He was going on about Jesus, about what he did for us by dying on the cross. I started to become interested in what he was saying. I had never heard it explained in this way before. He was saying all the things I've ever done wrong have already been atoned for by a man named Jesus Christ.

If only it were true, I thought. *If he had any idea how bad I am, how many things I've done wrong and how many people I've let down, he wouldn't be saying this.*

BELIEVE IN ME

Then suddenly, he was looking right at me! In this room, where there must have been at least 300 people, somehow, he decided to look me right in the face.

"You are saved," he asserted.

"Say a prayer from your heart, and God will answer you and tell you it's true. All you've ever done is forgiven."

I was transfixed, and at the same time, my heart was praying that what he was saying was true. Suddenly, I felt the answer; I knew he was right. I couldn't believe it could be true, but it was. I could feel it. It was the greatest feeling I'd ever known.

There were lines of mascara all the way down to my chin, and I still couldn't hold in my tears — they were gushing out. I hadn't realized how much pain I was carrying inside me. Now that I knew the truth, all of it was pouring out of me, and in its place was incredible joy and peace, filling me up until I thought I would burst.

***

I wandered into the house I shared with Jim. "Hi, Jim, I'm home." He said nothing. He was sitting in front of the television, as usual.

Will he remember? Will he say anything?

God, if Jim remembers my birthday, I'll take it as a sign that everything is going to be fine, that he really cares for me.

But I could see from the start that either Jim had forgotten or he didn't care.

SUFFICIENT TO **STAND**

I can't go on like this.

I met Jim through the church and he helped me so much in those first days after I accepted Jesus as my Savior. Without him, I don't know if I would have been able to drop alcohol and drugs from my life so completely. I fell in love with Jim, gave him more than a year of my life and gave birth to his son. But still, he wouldn't marry me and didn't want anyone to know he was the father. I had to face the fact that he never really cared. I just wasn't good enough for him or his millionaire family. Now, I was once again being rejected by someone I loved.

Is there such a thing as love? God, have you rejected me, too?

Suddenly, I was overcome with hopelessness. I had been so strong, and I thought I was doing everything right. I quit drinking, quit smoking, quit going out. I gave my all to Jim, did everything for him. Now I had no money of my own, no job, no home and an infant son to take care of. I was afraid to go to my parents' home, afraid that in my devastated state, I would fall back into my dependence on pot. I had nowhere to go, and I hadn't slept in days. I went upstairs, fingered through the cabinets in the bathroom and swallowed a handful of Percocet. Then I threw myself on my bed.

After lying there several minutes, I realized what I had done. I sped to the bathroom to see if I had really ingested so many pills. The bottle was empty. Already I could feel a haze enveloping me. It felt as if I were floating through clouds. I lay back down. To be finally at rest felt so good; I couldn't fight it. I left a message for Drew, telling him how much I loved him. Then I closed my eyes.

I can't believe this is the end.

Suddenly, through the fog surrounding my head, I heard a voice.

I will take care of you if you will help me, but you have to believe in me, you have to trust me.

I knew it was God, and I did believe.

I answered, *Please show me how! I need a home, and I need money to take care of my children. Show me how. Please don't give up on me, God; I want to live for you.*

Again, I heard the voice: *Believe.*

My body was already numb, my mind practically asleep. It took every last bit of effort to move myself out of the bed and down the stairs. But I didn't give up.

***

"Amy, I have to tell you something."

I looked at my dad, a bit nervous about what he would say. I still couldn't quite believe what had happened that day. I convinced my entire family, my brother, my sister and her family, my two sons, my mother and even my father, who has never believed in God, to accompany me to Easter service at Friends Church. It was the first time we had ever gone to church as a family. They even seemed to enjoy it. I wasn't sure, though.

"Amy, I can't believe the change I see in you." I was about to protest. I was sure he was about to criticize my

SUFFICIENT TO **STAND**

involvement with the church. "I haven't seen you so happy since you were a child. And you've brought the whole family closer together. You going to this church has been the best thing that ever happened to this family."

I couldn't believe my ears. It was the kind of praise and attention I'd always craved from my father. And I knew I deserved it. I stifled a grateful tear. Over the last two years, I had overcome so much. After leaving Jim, I stayed two days in a homeless shelter with my infant son before finding the strength to return to my parents' house. Then Jim had tried to gain full custody of our son. This time, I didn't back down or give up through the whole two-year court battle, and I won shared custody. And the whole time, I stayed sober and clean; I never consumed so much as a sleeping pill.

It was Jesus that carried me through it all. Jesus who provided me the strength when it seemed certain I would lose my youngest son, or I could no longer resist the temptation to enjoy just one drink, one joint. He led me to a program called Celebrate Recovery that brought me back to life.

Celebrate Recovery is a ministry dedicated to fellowship and celebrating God's healing power through eight recovery principles. The program allowed me to become free of my addictive, compulsive and dysfunctional behaviors. The freedom I experienced through Celebrate Recovery has allowed me to experience peace, serenity, joy and a closer and deeper relationship with God. This is the program that started me on the road to entrusting my life

BELIEVE IN ME

completely to God.

As my faith grew, I also became more involved in the church, and I found acceptance and a love that made me stronger than ever. Soon, I was leading prayer and small groups; my longtime fear of being accepted by others had been conquered.

Now, I had come full circle. My father was standing before me with a look of love and admiration in his eyes, while the rest of my family looked on happily. I took my sons' hands and led them all to our Easter dinner.

***

Every morning, I wake up and recite Jeremiah 29:11: "For I know the plans the Lord has for me." I ask the Holy Spirit to guide me through the day, reveal to me the Lord's plan. And as I go through the day, I can sense Jesus watching over me and feel his hand leading me. I know he has a purpose for me, and that all I went through, all the mistakes I made, only prepared me for that purpose. He has even provided for me, the way he promised he would.

Now, I have my own cabin, a car that starts and is warm in the winter and, most important of all, time to spend with my two sons. It's a very simple life — we don't even have running water. But it is the most fulfilling life I've ever known. I enjoy things I never thought I would be able to enjoy again — swimming, hiking cross country, even cleaning my little cabin in the woods. I have not dated since my relationship ended with Jim. My life is my

SUFFICIENT TO **STAND**

children, fellowship with others at my church and God.

I can now speak about my past without feeling the remorse I once did, and I use it to help others. I am in a small group at Friends Church and, through God working in me at Celebrate Recovery, I try to help others who may feel the same way I once did — that they are bad inside, that they will never be forgiven or accepted. I want them to know how much Jesus loves them and how much he is willing to do for them, if they only believe.

CONCLUSION

Genesis states: "You were made in the image of God." How are you like God? God gave you a choice. You can choose good or bad, right or wrong, life or death, admit you have a problem or ignore it. God says, "You can reject me or accept me. It's your choice." You can choose to face your problem or not.

Free will is not only a blessing, it's also a burden, because sometimes we make bad choices. And the bad choices cause all kinds of painful consequences in our lives.

I can choose to experiment with drugs; if I get addicted, it's my fault. I can choose to be sexually promiscuous; if I get a disease, it's my fault. God says, "No, I don't want you to have this pain, but it's part of the package that is free will."

What's the antidote to denial? What makes me finally face up to my problems?

God's antidote for denial is pain. We rarely change when we see the light; we change when we feel the heat. We don't change until our fear of change is exceeded by the pain. Most people don't move into recovery until they're forced to move into it because there is no other option.

You see the dilemma? With free will, we receive blessings, but we also get a burden. And God says, "I'm not going to overrule your will." God doesn't send anybody to

SUFFICIENT TO **STAND**

hell; you choose to go there by rejecting everything that he does. You may be choosing to live a preview as you stay in the throes of addiction.

He says, "I love you; I want you to be a part of my family."

If you say, "Forget it, God," thumb your nose and walk out the other door, you really can't blame anybody but yourself. There is free will.

Man is "Free to Fall," but he is also "Sufficient to Stand." That sufficiency comes when we choose the grace that is offered to us through Jesus Christ and the ministry of his church.

Paul asked God to remove "the thorn from my flesh."

God's answer is still the same: "My grace is sufficient for you."

Saved by His Grace

Jeff Wall
Pastor and fellow struggler

FRIENDS
COMMUNITY CHURCH

We would love for you to join us!
We meet Sunday mornings at 9 and 11 a.m. at
1485 30th Avenue, Fairbanks, AK 99701.

Please call us at 907.452.2249 for directions or
contact us at www.friendschurch.org.

For more information on reaching your city with
stories from your church, please contact
Good Catch Publishing at
www.goodcatchpublishing.com

GOOD CATCH
PUBLISHING

Did one of these stories touch you?
Did one of these real people move you to tears?
Tell us (and them) about it on our reader blog at
www.goodcatchpublishing.blogspot.com.